'And the skylight lets the moonlight in, and those Apples are deep-sea apples of green' (John Drinkwater)

Maureen McBain was almost an 'only child'. She remembers being banished to sleep one evening in the apple loft. There were strange voices below, but nobody told her a baby brother had been born and died. By the time a small sister arrived seven years later she felt almost grown up. She had discovered the magic of words, the joy of growing flowers in her own small corner of the garden. And the haunting sound of the waves lapping the shingle.

As a volunteer for the WRNS, her first posting was to a Dover Coastal Forces base operating under shellfire. When the MTB flotillas moved after D Day the Wrens went with them to Ramsgate, under the flight path from Manston RAF airfield. The sense of comradeship was cemented some 50 years later by the White Cliffs Service of Thanksgiving at St Mary's Parish Church, Dover, for 'All those who had fulfilled their duties' in Hellfire Corner.

As a UN wife 'in the field' she found the same sense of comradeship with problems shared. So the circle widened, and two small boys grew up with a mixed bag of friends and the universal language of childhood play.

She still enjoys scribbling, sharing home-grown apples with the blackbirds, and moonlight over the sea. Not too far from Dover.

THE LOCUST YEARS

Annals of a UN Wife

Maureen McBain

The Book Guild Ltd
Sussex, England

First published in Great Britain in 2002 by
The Book Guild Ltd
25 High Street,
Lewes, East Sussex
BN7 2LU

Copyright © Maureen McBain 2002

The right of Maureen McBain to be identified as the author of
this work has been asserted by her in accordance with the
Copyright, Designs and Patents Act 1988.

All rights reserved. No part of this publication may be
reproduced, transmitted, or stored in a retrieval system, in any form
or by any means, without permission in writing from the publisher,
nor be otherwise circulated in any form of binding or cover other
than that in which it is published and without a similar condition
being imposed on the subsequent purchaser.

Typesetting in Times by
Keyboard Services, Luton, Bedfordshire

Printed in Great Britain by
Athenaeum Press Ltd, Gateshead

A catalogue record for this book is available from
The British Library

ISBN 1 85776 641 5

CONTENTS

Acknowledgements		vi
Prologue		vii
1	China Bound	1
2	Austria	9
3	A Glimpse of Bangkok	14
4	Burma	17
5	India	21
6	Furlough and the Hills	26
7	Mustapha	34
8	Septembers	38
9	Mary	41
10	Sitaram	43
11	The Maldives	46
12	Pearl Garden	50
13	New York Remembered	60
14	Land of the Morning Calm	66
15	Home	77
16	Ethiopia	83
17	Farewell to Chosun	106
Epilogue		109

ACKNOWLEDGEMENTS

My heartfelt thanks to long-time friends David and Doreen for their support and encouragement, and to the younger generation, especially Richard and Lindy, for their expertise freely shared in my endless wars with the word processor.

Without them this book would never have been finished.

PROLOGUE

On the seashore of endless worlds children meet. Tempest roams in the pathless sky, ships are wrecked in the trackless water, death is abroad and the children play.

Rabindranath Tagore

From *The Crescent Moon*

I was privileged to be a 'UN wife' for some 40 years; mostly with UNICEF, in those pioneer years devoted to the battle with disease and malnutrition prevalent among half the world's children. I have called them the 'locust years' because we were so busy living them that we did not have time to notice their passing.

This book is to record some of those memories while time remains, as a tribute to my husband, whose life it was, and to friends and colleagues in UNICEF and the other UN agencies working together in humanitarian projects who became our family in those early days 'in the field'. Their friendship, their loyalty and quiet dedication incur a debt of gratitude.

Memories also remain of so many who smoothed the path of the two strangers in their country with their kindness and unbelievable tolerance. They too were our friends, and very much part of our family.

1

China Bound

I took a slow boat to China and arrived in the middle of a revolution and Chinese New Year.

We had announced our engagement after a performance of Beethoven's Pastoral Symphony by the Bournemouth Philharmonic Orchestra at the Pavilion, in September 1946. I remember it clearly because I felt very thirsty afterwards. The milk bars were all closed, it had started to rain, and there were no taxis. So our first concert together was not all wine and roses. Both families had been evacuated to Bournemouth during the war with the London bank where our respective fathers pursued their mysterious Home Guard activities with great enthusiasm after office hours.

I was in the Wrens operating a 35-mm projector showing educational and entertainment films to audiences of MTB (motor torpedo boat) crews of the Dutch, Norwegian and British naval flotillas in between their 'routine' operational sorties in the Dover Straits. The 'Careless Talk Costs Lives' and 'In Which We Serve' movies are still imprinted in my memory. The sailors preferred Betty Grable.

Alan was in China driving trucks laden with medical supplies along the Burma Road, so we had not seen much of each other since 1939. That was not unusual during those war years when lives tended to be topsy-turvy. But both families seemed pleased when we told them our news and we planned a spring wedding in England on his next return from China following an assignment with IRO (International Refugee Organisation, later to be reborn in the United Nations High

Commission for Refugees) in Shanghai. Their urgent mission at that time was to 'resettle' as many as possible of the White Russian refugees who had flooded down originally from Harbin, to Tientsin and Nanking and finally Shanghai, in the new worlds of Australasia, Canada or America.

Time passed. We must have spent a small fortune on postage. News from China on radio and in newspapers was scant with so much happening at home and in Europe. Then in late autumn 1948 a series of articles in my uncle's favourite newspaper (he liked the crossword) featured the 'Five Threatened Cities' of China as the Red Armies were marching south. Incoming letters became even less punctual. Then a cable arrived from Shanghai: 'Regret home leave postponed due heavy workload. Can you book passage here? Letter follows. Love.'

My uncle, despite serious misgivings on the wisdom of the move, managed to fix a passage from Southampton to Hongkong on the SS *Canton* ... sailings were still few and far between in those early post-war years. The agents could not book a firm onward reservation to Shanghai but gave me a written request for a berth on the SS *Shenking* to be confirmed on arrival in Hongkong.

The four weeks on board were sheer bliss. Beyond the bustle of Port Said and Aden the empty sea stretched to a blue horizon that changed with every shifting cloud, the only sound was the chugging of engines and lap of waves; I don't remember any 'entertainment'. I think we played deck quoits. Mostly we just watched the creamy wake lengthen and melt in the distance. The silence was haunting. We reached Bombay just before daylight and the smell drifted over the still dark water as I watched the shore lights coming closer. The steamy smell of spice, jasmin, people and dust was India; the beginning of a heart-tug that has lasted a lifetime.

We disembarked in Hongkong on a Saturday, and a message was waiting. An office colleague on a brief assignment to Hongkong would be meeting me to help in any way he could, and to see me safely aboard on the last lap of the journey. So I set off for the agents' office.

They confirmed my booking on a small coastal steamer called the *Shenking*, and said they were just closing for Race Week but to pick up my ticket to embark the following Saturday. There was a letter for me from Alan's colleague. He had been sent unexpectedly to Macao the day before and was writing to say how sorry he was to miss me, but to make use of his hotel room while in Hongkong. He enclosed the key.

I made my way to the little 'creamery' where my late cabin mates had arranged to meet me for tea. Mary and Clare were Irish nurses on their way to open a new TB sanatorium in the Wanchai district with the young nun who was to be the doctor in charge. She was horrified when I read them the note. 'You could be risking your immortal soul,' she said firmly. 'A strange man's room in a Chinese hotel? Oh no ... you're coming with us.' They had no patients as yet, and at that time all the senior police and Customs officers in Hongkong, and the priests, who knew every nook and cranny of the by-ways, seemed to be Irish Catholic too. So we had a wonderful week being guided round the sights and the Chinese eating-places. The week flew past. They waved goodbye as I finally boarded the SS *Shenking* in bright January sunshine. It looked very small and vulnerable after the *Canton*.

The weather changed as we sailed north. Most of the passengers were Chinese, intent on settling themselves and vast piles of baggage safely below, and they seldom reappeared except for meals, so I had the upper deck very much to myself as the wind began to freshen and the waves heaved the little craft round in ever steeper furrows. There were glimpses of flying fish, and with sunset and moonrise the dark waters were fluorescent-tipped.

The first glimpse of mainland China on the third day had an air of unreality. As the waterfront drew closer you could identify the famous Bund, the Customs clocktower and dome, the Hongkong and Shanghai Bank, and the British Club with the longest bar in the world (where no female was allowed entry), all set in immaculate lawns with familiar trees and more reminiscent of London than the distant land of Cathay.

In fact everything about that year was unreal. There were the dragon dances and fireworks to celebrate Chinese New Year. Then came a simple wedding ceremony solemnised by the Canadian Dean with organ music played by the Chinese lady organist of Shanghai Anglican Cathedral. On a brief honeymoon in Taiwan, we travelled in bucket seats round the sides of a cargo plane loaded with livestock, and hessian-wrapped mountains of anonymous baggage filling the centre section.

Back in Shanghai we began married life in a furnished penthouse apartment in Avenue Joffre in the heart of the once fashionable French Concession, in luxury undreamed of before or since. There were polished parquet floors, display cabinets filled with jade and carved ivory, classic furniture, and a roof garden with a wonderful view across the city. The rent was unbelievably low because the businessman who owned it had evacuated his family to safer climes and was anxious for it to be occupied. It came with resident 'house boy' who had his own room across the landing from the front door. He spoke little English but made his disapproval quite clear. We soon discovered we had disturbed his sideline of rearing golden carp in preparation for the Moon Festival in our bathroom. I have always wondered where they went next.

In the street below, crowds jostled past shop windows enticingly piled with bales of rich silks and brocades, carved furniture and camphor-wood chests, antique scrolls and paintings, jewelry and baubles. Further on were the Chinese pharmacies, their shelves crammed with herbal remedies, Tiger balm, powdered rhino horn, and tall jars filled with pickled snake, ginseng roots, and the shrivelled anatomical specimens of I knew not what, lovingly preserved. Street stalls piled with oriental fruits and strange vegetables, live chickens strung up by the legs, sweetmeats and honeycomb nudged for space with the food sellers' cauldrons of steaming noodles and rice, dimsum dumplings filled with pork and ginger, crispy seaweed and fried prawns, and my favourite, *utiya* ... a sort of crunchy stick of sweet-coated cereal to be chewed or dunked. And amidst it all were the beggars, the shoeshine boys, the rickshaw boys, and once an elderly White Russian lady selling matches.

There were visiting naval ships in those early days whose crews were entertained by residents and returned the hospitality aboard. I recall HMS *Belfast* and the Australian Navy's *Shoalhaven* moored offshore with lights ablaze, welcoming guests to parties the same evening ... the *Belfast*, a formal white-tie occasion with VIPs piped aboard, and the *Shoalhaven* a cheerful beer and bangers affair. We were on the *Shoalhaven*.

The HMS *Amethyst* story was quite different. She was caught in the crossfire between the opposing armies on either side of the Yangtse river. On April 25 the cathedral was full, this time for a service in memory of the 44 crew members who died. On the same day came news of the fall of Nanking, reputedly without a shot being fired, and the march south began. We waited anxiously for news of the little *Amethyst*, trapped and we knew not how badly damaged. None came.

The urgent evacuation of remaining refugees, of whom the 'hard core' now housed in the TB Sanatorium were the most vulnerable, was now top priority. Office hours grew longer and more pressured. As villagers from the surrounding countryside flooded in with their pathetic bundles of belongings by bicycle, cart, rickshaw or on foot to seek safety in the city, city dwellers trying to leave were being delayed by the Nationalist army and gendarmerie checking papers and baggage, so chaos and confusion jammed all roads. A curfew was enforced from 10 p.m. to 6 a.m. The Embassy advised all British citizens who were 'staying put' to keep a reserve of candles and water, and buckets of sand in case of fire. Rumours grew of a defensive wooden wall being hastily erected on the outskirts of the city.

On May 25 I woke early. Curfew was now between 8 p.m. and 5.30 a.m., and all public transport banned from 6 p.m., so the noise was unusual. We watched from the roof garden. The last bewildered remnants of the Nationalist army seemed to be making their way slowly towards the waterfront ... like the villagers, by any means available but mostly, wearily, on foot. We noticed three armoured cars abandoned by the roadside had been hastily decked with improvised banners of greeting to 'Our Liberators' and as we watched, a group of small children clambered aboard and began happily playing soldiers in their new toy. Otherwise the road was now empty and it was very quiet.

Then, almost indistinguishable except for uniforms in a slightly lighter shade of khaki, the advance guard of the 'People's army' marched quietly past below. The children went on playing. The office and all the shops remained closed. We enjoyed the unusual luxury of doing nothing in the sunshine on the roof garden. Followed a period of almost 'normal' life, except that mail was irregular if it came at all because the airport was closed and the Nationalist navy was blockading the port, so little slipped in by sea. The house boy disappeared overnight, taking the contents of the room across the landing with him. Everything was orderly and shops came to life again, but it was quiet in the streets.

Then came a buzz of excitement as news seeped through of the dramatic escape of the little *Amethyst* with her surviving crew, slipping quietly down the Yangtse under cover of night to safety. All the Wren blood in my veins wanted to raise the Union Jack above the roof garden and yell for joy, but wiser counsel and my service training (Careless Talk Costs Lives) prevailed. Instead there were quiet prayers of thanksgiving in the Shanghai Anglican Cathedral and we all wished her safe passage home.

The office drivers went on strike for better conditions and pay, and took their case to the People's Tribunal, who unexpectedly moved that they were overpaid anyway. So they went back to work. But it became increasingly difficult to run the office with minimal communication with headquarters and the outside world. The powers that be decided the foreign staff should be re-assigned and the senior Chinese staff left in charge. We all waited and hoped.

Suddenly Nina appeared. She was a White Russian ex-ballerina who needed money while awaiting a passage to Australia, and decided to work for us. She polished the parquet floor to within an inch of its life while practising pirouettes with her mop. She fed us with home-cooked borsch and cabbage, scrubbed the kitchen and washed everything within sight. For some reason she displayed a fierce loyalty to the British in general and us in particular which would have struck terror into the heart of any would-be intruder. Finally word came of our re-assignment to Austria. We queued like everyone else for exit permits. Ours took three days, during which time anyone with a claim against the applicant could delay authorisation until the 'debt' was paid. We were lucky that no-one did. Perhaps Nina scared them off. Then word came by the grapevine that the *Maréchal Joffre* was on her way.

She was a French naval vessel delegated to conduct the French Ambassador to Hongkong and with him any French citizens who wished to leave. The remaining space was to be offered to non-French nationals. We had orders to pack and stand by, so we did. We also had a farewell party with the leftover drinks. Alan showed unexpected talent in mixing a very potable cocktail using all available bottles, and Nina had the first sip. Her comment in thick Russian accent pronounced it 'No good ... I can still see.' She added more vodka.

It was a mixed gathering of friends ... Chinese, German, Russian, Scandinavian, American, Australian, British and Turko-Tartar, all part of a very real bond of hopes and loyalties and of problems shared with which I grew familiar over the years.

At the dockside the following morning, passengers were all searched before boarding. My Chinese friend Nancy rushed up the gang plank with the farewell present of a basket of persimmons. So that was searched too. Then the Communist Seamen's Union paid a farewell tribute to the French Seamen's Union crew members with music and waving of flags as the anchor was raised and we steamed out of harbour very slowly.

It must have been around midnight when the ship's engines suddenly stopped. The commanding officer of the Nationalist naval contingent manning the blockade wished to pay his respects to the French Ambassador, who had retired for the night but reciprocated with typical Gallic charm and courtesy. After that the three-day voyage was uneventful.

It was many moons later when we heard that Simon, the ship's cat serving on the *Amethyst*, had been posthumously awarded the feline equivalent of the Victoria Cross for devotion to duty under fire. Although wounded by a shell splinter, he had kept the ship's dwindling food supply safe from rats.

2

Austria

Austria was another world.

We reached Vienna by train after a brief reunion with our families in England. I had the upper bunk in a two-berth sleeper after boarding in Calais, and unwisely opened the window for fresh air, then slept soundly as we rattled through the night. I woke feeling chilly and in need of a cup of hot tea. Peering below, I could distinguish a hump of blankets covered in a light powdering of snow, and Alan's face emerged scowling and quite blue with cold. The cool fresh air which had soothed me to sleep had deflected in a down draught. It was obviously not the right moment to suggest he went in search of tea.

Our new posting was to Kapfenberg refugee camp in Steiermark. Post-war Austria was divided into four zones administered by the Allied powers, America, Russia, France and England, and we were bound for the British zone. We changed trains in Vienna ... a sprawling barn of a station with glass still missing from the roof and a confusion of steam and hurrying passengers and booming announcements of arrivals and departures, most of which we did not understand, in the chill early morning light. Still no comforting hot tea.

Our ongoing journey took us through the unspoilt mountain scenery of the Russian zone, over the Semmering pass with check points for examination of documents by first Russian and then British border guards, to the sleepy village of Kindberg, where a room in a small *gasthaus* was our new home. The bedroom was clean scrubbed wood, the walls decorated with edelweiss and gentian frescoes in white and blue. The double bed was buried under an enormously heavy, smothering eiderdown, and there was a round wooden table in a sunny alcove, an electric ring, and a wash basin. The one toilet, reached by a creaky wooden staircase to the landing below, was shared by residents and locals frequenting the bar. We found on Saturday evenings it tended to be disconcertingly popular.

We had a large latticed window overlooking the garden and the pigsty, and the gate led straight into a winding path up a forested slope where I would glimpse the occasional wild fawn on early morning walks. I did a lot of walking in between Alan's departure for the camp in the morning and his return in the early evening. The mountain meadows were dazzling under the first cover of snow in brilliant sunshine, and the quietness muffled the small noises in the woods. There were little wooden shrines, always simply decorated with woodland flowers or greenery, in unexpected corners. Sometimes I would encounter a lone woodcutter, or a hunter in pursuit of rabbit or wild fowl for the family pot, who would greet the English stranger with a smile and '*Grüss Gott*' in passing. But mostly I had those quiet woods to myself, which was magical after the hustle and bustle of city streets.

In that part of Austria the men tended to wear the local dress of lederhosen, forest-green jackets and a hat decorated with a quill. The larger the feather, the more skilled the hunter was presumed to be. The women reserved their costumes, with starched white embroidered blouses and bonnets, black velvet-laced high waistcoats and flowing skirts, for Sunday's churchgoing and high days and holidays. I practised the German vaguely remembered from school days and the village folk were very friendly and tolerant of my mistakes. In fact they were friendly and tolerant towards us all and our strange foreign ways.

There were two staff members with the same surname, one Russian and one Swiss, and with a shared passion for fishing the trout so abundant in the local river. They were overheard one evening discussing their catch. One extra-large fish excited Vassily's close interest.

'Which fly you used?' he asked. Kurt shook his head. 'No fly. But a wurm.' 'Mit a wurm?' said Vassily disapprovingly. 'But that's not crickets.' After that they became known as the 'Breetish Element'.

The camp 'commandant' and senior officer was South African. Leo was a massive man with a booming voice, a heart of gold and a beloved 'hunting dog' called IRO, a spaniel with huge pleading eyes and an insatiable appetite for the sugary confections from the local bakery he was forbidden to eat but managed to scrounge when his master's attention was diverted. Each morning, the inseparable twosome would stride across the village square after a hearty breakfast towards their waiting jeep. One morning it failed to start. Repeated efforts resulted in a very choked engine sound. The Austrian driver leapt to his feet as a command echoed round the square. 'Alfred, *gehen Sie unter das* car und find out was *ist das* noise und come back *schnell*.' Alfred did that. I asked him once whether he understood what the Colonel said. 'No,' he answered, 'but I always know what he means.'

The camp housed refugees from Yugoslavia, Rumania, Hungary and Czechoslovakia, all apparently speaking each other's languages, as well as German, fluently. Their English seemed to improve daily too, which was disconcerting in view of my fractured efforts with German. They were serious music lovers and would sometimes invite us to evening gatherings to share their favourite melodies and ethnic dances and drink freshly brewed Austrian beer. A large Hungarian couple were professional weight-lifters as well as musicians. They would swing heavy wooden tables and benches around with one hand. When they quarrelled, everyone dived for cover. When they played Liszt, their violin strings could cry. Perhaps it was their way of grieving for the homeland they loved.

Each had their own tragic story of loss and helplessness in the isolation of devastation that follows in the wake of every war. This UN operation could only try to facilitate their 'resettlement' – such a cold word for adapting to a whole new world from the one where they had once been warm and safe and loved – in a country where their talents and skills could be used again and that basic human need of dignity and self-respect restored. The visiting 'teams' from the host countries worked very hard to do that. Many of the refugees were success stories again in their new lives on the other side of the world. A few of them kept in touch by letter over the years and it was so good to sense their pride in a treasured new home and job. But it cannot have been easy.

Our weekends were usually free and we spent them trudging up the curving woodcutters' tracks through the pine-forested slopes of the nearby mountains, always to find a small inn at the summit with a massive wood-burning stove providing smoked garlic sausage and rich salty ham, served with freshly baked *schwarzbrot* and schnapps. The hot chocolate was warming too. Some of Alan's colleagues went further afield to the ski slopes. We tried it, but the Austrian leather boots were heavy and blister-making, hired skis in those days enormously long and unwieldy, and one spent more time scrambling back up icy slopes than on the brief descent. The local children seemed to have no such problem, and four-year-olds would whizz past with unerring skill as we ineptly slithered in their way, which was less than encouraging. But the air was pine-laden and sweet and the sun always seemed to shine. Spring came, with fruit blossoms and streams brimming with melted snow. Summer brought the wild strawberries and mountain meadows knee-high with wild flowers.

From the outside world came rumours of mounting problems as governments struggled with attempted solutions to the reconstruction of war-shattered economies, the discontent and the broken promises The post-war world was becoming 'tired of the refugee problem', and as months passed, the familiar UN story of insufficient resources made everyone's future insecure. In September, out of the blue, a telegram arrived from UNICEF Asia Regional Office offering Alan a job as Program Officer, with an urgent assignment dependent on his early arrival in Bangkok.

So we packed once again.

3

A Glimpse of Bangkok

September 1950 found us hurtling across Europe again, this time in a little Austin Devon. We spent two days staying with parents, and made a hurried foray to the London shops in search of tropical clothing, without much success. The summer sales were over, and normal customers were buying autumn tweeds and winter boots. But we were treated tolerantly and with unusual deference and I wondered why. 'They think it's real mink,' Alan said, pointing to my coat. I looked down, remembered the Chinese girl friend in Shanghai who had guided me through the intricacies of the bargaining technique essential for market shopping and breathed a silent thank you ... Nancy had located this mink-looking Chinese 'coney' for sale by her tailor at, she said, an unbelievably low price and insisted we must buy it for those terrible European winters. Alan had agreed somewhat reluctantly. It had indeed been reassuringly light and warm in the Austrian snows, I had never owned a fur coat before, and it was like parting with an old friend when my mother offered to look after it for my return. Those were the primitive days when we still used the skins as well as eating rabbits.

We were met at Bangkok airport by an office car. On the journey into town the driver casually avoided three large but unhurried snakes ... obviously a regular procedure which I tried not to think about. Accommodation had been arranged in a house quite close to the office, the Thai equivalent of a bed and breakfast, and the smiling Thai lady owner was waiting to greet us. Our bedroom overlooked the walled garden, where a shrine with a small statue of the Buddha was garlanded daily with fresh jasmin. There was a power cut that evening (not unusual in those pre-tourist days) so the ceiling fan didn't work. A giant spider gave birth to a brood of horribly active young on the landing outside as I made my way back from the bathroom. Alan had come armed with an emergency can of insecticide (a lifelong habit from his wartime Burma Road days), so we closed the bedroom door firmly and we slept.

Breakfast was always cool papaya sprinkled with fresh lime juice. Our Thai hostess would prepare lunch when we needed it ... hot soup and a bowl of tropical fruit, where I encountered custard apple and durian for the first time. While Alan was working I explored the street markets and managed to find cotton shifts and bush shirts to augment our scanty tropical wardrobe. When not with office colleagues, who were very generous in entertaining us in their homes or showing us the local sights, we enjoyed exploring the evening scene. For some reason, every dish on the menu of the few Western-style hotels tasted the same – of Maggie sauce. So we ate at the local eating houses. Our favourite was a Chinese restaurant where the chairs and tables on the pavement were shaded by a canvas awning supported on pillars. There was a cheerful noise and clatter from the cooking area, the smell of hot charcoal and cooking oil, steaming rice and noodles, and always a faint overlay of garlic and jasmin on the humid evening air. The pillar next to our table was the haunt of a large gecko lizard who moved quite silently, to dart at sudden lightning speed to trap his supper of the juicier bugs, which he gulped down with closed eyes and obvious relish. Our meal was always delicious too.

Memories of our stay grow hazy now and a little unreal. Curtains drawn all daytime to shield rooms from the midday heat. The blinding glare of pavements and the heavy damp. The crescendo of traffic horns and rickshaw bells, and the sudden green quiet of the holy places, the monks in saffron robes, and the cool marble of the temples. There was always the fragrance of frangipani, the temple tree.

And the slender grace of the women's hands. Hands folded in prayer, hands cupped round flickering candlelights like moths' wings. We drew bamboo sticks in the temple to learn our fortune. They omitted to tell us of our imminent departure.

To Rangoon.

4

Burma

The sudden posting was completely unexpected. Alan was asked to leave urgently for Rangoon to establish a UNICEF office there. The Burmese government would provide office space and secretarial assistance. I could stay on in Bangkok until his return. Since we did not know when that would be, and Christmas was not that far away on the horizon, we decided I would come anyway. We managed to scrape together my fare, and my little portable typewriter travelled free, sharing my seat on the plane.

Burma in 1950 was still suffering from the aftermath of war, the Japanese occupation and the final struggles of the Allied armies' long march to retake Rangoon. There was unrest, and periodic skirmishes between the hill tribes and the government. The Karens and Kachins were renowned for their military prowess during the wartime campaign led by General Wingate, and now they wanted a degree of autonomy and were prepared to fight for it. Aung San, the Burmese nationalist leader and hero instrumental in securing Burmese independence, had tragically been assassinated in July 1947. Burma was a troubled country.

The capital, Rangoon, was a sad place. The Strand hotel – I think the only hotel – had all the forlorn trappings of its earlier luxury: faded brocade curtains and dusty chandeliers in the vast lounge bar, where an interesting collection of insects who had escaped the ceiling lizards dropped among the potted palms. On our first evening there the electricity seemed to be off more than on, so the ceiling fans were still and silent. But there was a Steinway piano with a hauntingly sweet tone and a Hungarian pianist. He played the 'Swan of Tuonela' in the empty room as if in his own little world. We thanked him and bought him a drink. Then we went to bed. Our bedroom had a stone balcony overlooking the main street, and we discovered our neighbour with the adjoining balcony was Percy Wood, the *New York Times* correspondent, on his way back from the Korean war front, where despatches, he told us, were winged home by the one working telephone shared with, among many others, Randolph Churchill. All this over our respective after-breakfast cigarette the following morning before setting off on our first foray into the city to locate the Health Ministry.

Beyond the wide stone steps from the hotel, the pavements were grubby and uneven, the few shops had little to sell, and the side streets seemed deserted apart from abandoned rubbish. There was an uneasy quietness in the air as we walked to find our daytime office in the Health Ministry. It turned out to be a small alcove in a room used apparently for storing files, which packed the wall shelves to ceiling height. We had a desk with a fan and an ancient 'sit up and beg' typewriter, two chairs and lots of paper. The Ministry officials were friendly and helpful, and slightly embarrassed about the apparent absence of secretarial help. So I took over the typing. The ancient machine became quite friendly in time, but the only fan was a hazard. Just at desk height, it managed to gobble up a long report in sextuplet which Alan dictated the following day. Our evening office was the hotel bedroom with my little portable. Meanwhile, the Ministry officials were busily arranging transport and visits to projects which might need and qualify for UNICEF help, so a sort of team-working system was established.

The first assignment was to an orphanage, where the children were lined up to greet us, all neatly dressed, clean and tidy, but with that passivity in their eyes that tugged at the heart strings and with which I became familiar over the years in other orphanages in Third World countries. I suppose they were not unlike our own orphanages in earlier days... A

MCH (Mother and Child Health) Centre was next, where the equipment was pitifully sparse for the orderly mass of patients in the hot little room.

It was the Children's Hospital that stayed in my mind although the visit remains a memory of fragments like an old movie run too fast: babies with limbs brittle like small birds', a little boy hollow-eyed with dysentery and fever, corridors with sick children in makeshift cots because there was no other room. But the most real of them still is the little Karen girl, an orphan whose parents had died somewhere along the road and who was found roaming the city streets starving and dazed, clutching her one possession ... a tiny, empty wooden box. She was bathed and fed and clothed, but no power on earth could part her from that little wooden box and she was clutching it fiercely as she slept. I recalled stories of the loyalty and devotion of Karen nurses behind the Japanese lines and wondered how it all made sense.

We were honoured to meet Madame Aung San, widow of the national hero, and a gracious lady still very involved with helping to alleviate poverty and sickness as her husband had been. She had invited us for lunch at her house by the lake. It was airy and cool with a light breeze rippling the water. Her daughter Aung San Suu Kyi must have been two years old then. We did not see her or her brothers, nor did we know then that she would follow her father's footsteps with the same unswerving devotion to her country whatever the cost. But we still treasure the memory of that occasion in a watercolour of the lake adjoining the house, with the shining gold of the Shwe Dagon pagoda far on the other side of the water.

The Burmese people were incredible. They had so many problems, but they were smiling and friendly, with a natural dignity which had little to do with worldly possessions or status. The Health Minister took the trouble to collect us soon after dawn one morning to show us the Shwe Dagon pagoda before the sun made the marble uncomfortably hot for Western feet. It was crowded even at that early hour with local people, barefoot like us, laying fresh flowers at their special shrine, kneeling or prostrate in prayer, or just walking quietly. A saffron-robed Buddhist monk greeted us in perfect English and told us a little of the history of this great Buddhist temple. The gold leaf covering the dome has been donated over many years by the faithful giving thanks for prayers answered, and another layer is added every year. Crowning the dome is a 'diamond bud' encrusted with jewels and guarded by four little golden bells swaying in the wind. By legend, the bells are said to ring only when danger approaches. The pagoda is surrounded by a wide platform of Italian marble lined all round with temples, each with its glittering mosaic work and a golden statue of the Buddha with his lovely serene face. The temple was used by the Allied wounded as an emergency hospital at the end of the war. Our friend smiled as he said it was the best place for healing them. It was both the cleanest and the holiest. How could we disagree?

The lady superintendent of the General Hospital has since died, as sadly has Madame Aung San. But I shall always remember their hospitality, introducing us to Burmese food, which I have loved ever since. Luckily we found a Burmese friend in our next 'port of call' who kept a stock of the pungent fish sauce with a shrill odour that I quickly developed a taste for, and we would eat together when our husbands were away on field trips.

Alan finished his assignment and I typed the last pages of the report in our hotel bedroom. A cable had arrived. We took off with airbags packed with cotton bush shirts and shifts, and the indispensable typewriter, for what we thought was a three-month assignment in India.

5

India

After an air-conditioned flight and a rather bumpy landing at DumDum airport, we found ourselves back in familiar steamy heat, milling traffic, and the seemingly endless surge of humanity which overflows Calcutta. In the heart of the city the old Victorian buildings melded with improvised shacks and flimsy rooftop dwellings in the throbbing street life of this Bengali cultural centre. Alan used the stopover time to revisit old haunts with obvious delight and I clutched the seat straps in sheer terror as we shot through the traffic with a taxi driver obviously bent on suicide. Cars, bicycles, horse-drawn tongas, buses and clanging trams all managed somehow to avoid the holy cows and the overflow of people from the narrow pavements. The airport seemed quite peaceful in comparison.

We boarded the Indian Airlines flight for what turned out to be the first of many journeys over the endless variety of patchwork terrain floating below. This time we followed the path of the great river Ganges most of the way northward. Irrigated fields gave way to barren ravines and the hilltop fortresses of Rajasthan where the Rani of Jhansi had once led her army of Rajput warriors to victory, Then the scorched plains where Akhbar's Moghul capital of Fatephur Sikri still lies abandoned for lack of a water supply in the early sixteenth century. Some 20 miles on lies Agra, where Shah Jehan had 20,000 labourers beginning to build the Taj Mahal, which took 20 years to complete. A memorial to his favourite wife, Muntaz Mahal, it is still a shrine of breathtaking beauty.

Then villages and cultivated fields marked the approach to the capital. The sheer size of India is awe-inspiring.

We landed at Palam airport, Delhi, in the late afternoon chill of November 24, 1950, to be greeted by Glan Davies, the UNICEF Chief of Mission, and Sukhlal, the driver, and delivered to Maidens' Hotel, Old Delhi, in the ageing office Chevrolet. This was another world of well-groomed lawns and quiet gardens, close to the historic Ridge and the old Mutiny church. November in northern India can be quite cold, especially in the evening. We shivered in the vast dining room, where the ranks of senior and lesser servitors in white starched uniforms and turbans of size indicating their rank far outnumbered the guests. We felt seriously underdressed in crumpled tropical clothes but the staple 'foreign' evening meal of cream of tomato soup, boily-roast chicken and caramelly custard was warming. So was the kindness of our new boss and his Bengali wife Sujata, who had loaned us blankets and made us feel immediately like part of the family.

We slept peacefully that night under our borrowed blankets, blissfully unaware that all our worldly goods, enumerated in the shipping list as 'two steel trunks and one wooden box with padlock', were independently starting their own journey aboard the steamship *Benlawers* from London docks to the UNICEF Asia Regional Office, Phra Atit Road, Bangkok. Thence, as Alan noted tersely when pursuing them many moons later, to follow us in ever-increasing circles round the globe. But that comes much later in the story.

The UNICEF office for India, Afghanistan and Ceylon in those days was a small one. There were two international staff members and six local staff, including the driver and the office cleaner. UNICEF occupied a small section of the ground floor of Patiala House, adjoining the Regional Office of our colleagues of the World Health Organisation, who had the larger part. Equipment was basic. Heating in winter and air conditioning in summer were non-existent, but the marble floors, pillars and domed roof were superb. It was originally one of the palaces of the Maharaja of Patiala, a strikingly tall and handsome Sikh nobleman, who still retained the upper floors, which must have had a superb view across the *maidan* – a vast area of greensward intersected with rectangular lakes and fringed with trees, stretching all the way to India Gate and beyond, to the former Governor's residence, now Rashtrapati Bhavan, the Presidential Palace, which dominated the skyline at its crest.

Secretarial help in the office was in short supply, so my little portable typewriter was still in demand to meet the inevitable 'deadlines'. We often took along sandwiches and a thermos of tea for lunch on the grass under the trees on those sunny winter days, while the shipping clerk, who was a high-caste Brahmin, put us to shame by having his lunch served hot from a highly polished brass tiffin carrier by his personal servant, who of course wore spotless uniform and a magnificent turban.

In our first two years in India, we moved 'home' eight times. From the Victorian splendour of Maidens' Hotel we found ourselves in a bed-sitting room in the home of a delightful American dentist whose favourite occupation when not occupied with teeth was hunting with his friend the Maharaja of Bikaner in his domain on the edge of the Thar desert in Rajasthan. So the running of the house was left very much to the head 'bearer', a scowling individual with a fierce loyalty to the doctor but obvious distrust of everyone else in the house. He made it clear we should get our own, personal bearer, so we did – a tiny old man who appeared at the door one day with his 'chitties'. These are testimonials from previous employers, often yellow and crumpled, but cherished tenderly, usually in a brown paper bag, without which no self-respecting household servant in India ever applies for a job. They extolled his virtues as a cook. He looked a little like Old Man Tortoise, in a uniform with an over-large collar to the jacket in which his neck appeared lost. He confided much later that he had one cracked and one broken ear drum so his hearing was not very reliable. But he was very willing. Mostly he occupied himself dusting, and the head bearer seemed to approve.

'The doc's' bungalow in Ferozshah Road was spacious and surrounded by a large mature garden in one of the quiet, tree-lined avenues leading to the *maidan*. Most of the other houses were occupied by government ministers, so we were in very august company. Our bedroom had double doors opening to the garden, a lofty ceiling with overhead *punkah*, and walls lined with *almirahs*, tall white cupboards with glass panels and creaky doors which were the Indian equivalent of wardrobes and chests of drawers combined. We had our own bathroom and small dressing room. The other paying guest was Peter, a young Lloyds Bank clerk who reminds me, now I come to think of it, of a young John McCarthy of hostage fame, with his boyish grin and easy sense of humour. Peter occupied similar accommodation across the hall, and we all breakfasted together. The head bearer presided grimly over the coffee percolator.

We started out sleeping on two ancient iron bedsteads with springs that had seen better days. One evening Alan had one of his furious bursts of activity and decided to dismantle them and reassemble them as a double divan. I declined to take any part in the operation, having suffered trapped fingers that way in the past, but I think I looked on helpfully. In the ensuing battle, bits of iron shot sideways and springs quivered protestingly. The peace of the night was finally shattered by a howl of rage and pain as one of the posts collapsed heavily and unexpectedly. The new bed proved quite comfortable once it had been supplemented by padded cotton overlay and colourful hand-printed bedcovers from the market. Thankfully the noise had not roused the household. Ferozshah Road was normally a very peaceful neighbourhood and even the jackals howled only in the distance.

In early March, Alan set off on field trips, first to Karachi and then to Bombay. He would be away for two weeks, so I decided it would be a good time to start learning some Hindi. A *munshi* was recommended, a nervous, bespectacled young man who came to the house each morning, and we embarked on the *Europeans' Guide to Hindustani in 36 Lessons*. It was a much-thumbed edition and contained a section on 'Medical and Military Phraseology' and another on 'Riding Lessons and Exercises', which I found utterly fascinating. 'Seyss, bring me my horse immediately' and 'When will your annual musketry be over?' might not have had immediate relevance but were an interesting glimpse of another era. Progress was not helped by Vicky, the dentist's fox terrier, who had taken it upon herself to become my guard dog and insisted on keeping me company during the day. This was not very popular with my long-suffering tutor, who did not share the Anglo-Saxon need of canine company. But we made quite a bit of progress between muted growls, and Vicky took to guarding me at night instead.

6

Furlough and the Hills

After Alan's return we managed our first visit to Agra, staying overnight in Lauries 'garden hotel' run by two Swiss ladies, the Hotz sisters. The sleeping accommodation was in individual small bungalows with front patios wreathed in the scarlet and purple-leafed tendrils of bougainvillaea, which grew everywhere. Everything was so pin-neat and reminiscent of Switzerland that it was almost unsurprising to find on the bedroom dressing table an embroidered pincushion containing two needles, one threaded with white and one with black cotton, two large and two small safety pins, and a darning needle. Alongside lay a small pair of scissors. The quiet gardens were bird-haunted and the leaves were wet with fresh rain. Our first glimpse of the Taj Mahal was just after a thunderstorm. The white marble glowed with a light all its own. The pearly iridescence was unbelievably beautiful against the glowering sky and the Jumna river beyond. We still have the photograph...

March ended with dust storms, and in April the temperature began to climb, the *maidan* grass looked dry and dusty, and in the doc's garden the brain fever bird began to sing. Glan was due to depart on home leave in June, and he suggested we snatch a break in the hills while there was time before Alan began preparing to take over as Acting Chief of Mission during his absence. So we set off in a borrowed Austin A40 for a weekend in Mussoorie, the nearest hill station.

It was a long drive, and we left soon after daybreak while

it was cool. Once over the Jumna bridge the road was fairly empty. We passed through the cantonment town of Meerut, then drove north all the way across the flat plains of the Ganges valley to Dehra Dun, where the road began to curve uphill through the forest reservation. With every mile the way grew steeper and more tortuous as the little Austin clung to the hairpin bends and I dared not look down. Up through heather-covered crags and pine-forested ravines the narrow curves seemed to be endless, until we reached a blessedly gentle incline and suddenly we were in the little town, which looked as though it had been sprinkled by a giant hand over the green foothills. Beyond stretched range upon range of grey mountain slopes, to reveal finally the shining snow peaks melting into a blue horizon. It was breathtaking.

The air was fresh and pine-scented. Transport from then on was by rickshaw pulled and pushed by five coolies, two in front and three behind for balance as they swung along the narrow tracks. The rickshaws congregated on the wide ridge at the end of the motor road leading to the Mall. In the days when the memsahibs took to the hill stations to escape the summer heat, many had had their own private rickshaws for transport to and from the bungalows nestling round the little town. These still had names echoing perhaps homes in the towns and villages they had left behind. Dingle Cottage, Ivy Cottage, Dulce Domum and Cosy Nook vied with Shamrock Cottage, Thistle Bank, Ivanhoe Cottage and Glen Rannock Lodge. The Mall had been the fashionable place to stroll and be seen after Sunday church or late on cool summer afternoons. It still boasted a flourishing library and City Hall, the Indian Theatre and Picture Palace, and a few of the smaller, respectable but faded hotels among the little shops selling groceries, hardware, leather goods and jewelry, as it wound its way up to Landour Bazaar. Signposts en route indicated directions to Gun Hill and the Polo Ground, Murray Spring Forest and the Kemti Falls, which were favourite picnic areas, and closer at hand the Happy Valley Tennis Club, Pleasure Valley and, intriguingly, Scandal Point.

We found the Savoy hotel and Dun View Cottage for the

first time and fell in love with it. A short distance from the main hotel building across rough grass and trees where the squirrels played, it was quite on its own overlooking the escarpment. Winding tracks followed the old horse and cart roads to the breweries, where excellent Indian beer is made from the clear spring waters, down to the Dun Valley. To the left was a tiny wooden balcony, facing the Himalayan ranges which stretched to the Tibetan and Nepalese borders beyond the clouds. The silence was awesome.

Away from the hotel, it was a joy to walk on mountain paths again with deep forested valleys dropping on one side and wild blue periwinkles, violets and wood anemones starring the mossy bank on the other. It was a little like the mountain paths of Steiermark, with the tinkling of bells from cattle cropping the rough grass of the pastures below. But this was wilder and more remote.

Just before sunset we found a winding path leading to a deserted house ... probably occupied every summer in days gone by. A child's toy still lay abandoned in the garden, where a path led across untended lawns to a huge flat-topped boulder. As we sat there watching, the panorama unfolded of ever more towering peaks, glimpsed through the shifting clouds as the sun dipped.

Back at Dun View Cottage we were still in time to watch the slow radiance of deepening pink melt into dove grey. The glow seemed to linger till the last on Trisul, the loveliest peak of them all.

As evening fell, small lights began to flicker in the Dun Valley below. Wafts of charcoal smoke mixed with spices drifted on the night wind from the village fires and then everything was quiet. A small bird called among the pine trees with a *chuk-chuk* cry – they said it was the Indian nightjar or *chiipak*, who moves almost silently with a moth-like flight hunting night insects – and we drifted into sleep. Tomorrow's journey back seemed a world away.

Back in Delhi, office work went on apace until departure day came and we wished the Davies family a safe flight home and a happy home leave in Wales. Projects initiated before Glan's departure were going well. Medical supplies and X-ray apparatus were already beginning to arrive in Bombay for distribution to the three new TB control centres, and skim-milk powder for the milk distribution scheme which preceded by some years the very successful dairy project at Anand. There the new milk sterilisation and bottling plant was to become a huge success commercially as well as health-wise, both for humans and for animals producing the milk, when the far-sighted Indian director introduced free veterinary treatment for the local farmers' cows and buffaloes. It was good to feel a small part in these beginnings. I know we both did, although through the long summer days the barometer crept relentlessly higher.

Towards the end of July the baobob, or monkey bread tree, burst into massive white flowers, which are said to open at midnight. By mid-morning the flowers wither, eventually to form the huge gourd-like fruit which poses a hazard to the unwary passer-by when it unexpectedly plummets to the ground and bursts. With August the temperature could reach 120°F at midday as the monsoon clouds massed closer and the air grew heavy and clammy. The rain always seemed a long time coming. But that first sudden ice-cold shower was magical. The torrent of heavy drops spattered the dust like vengeful bullets, and thunder rumbled round a suddenly darkening sky. This was the time when snakes surfaced on the golf course, and a tiny blue flower overnight covered the bare earth in nearby Lodhi Gardens. The children squealed with delight and came out to play in the new puddles.

I cannot remember the exact date when the Danes arrived. Poul Larsen was a welcome addition to the UNICEF office team He had been a kayak champion in the 1936 Olympic Games, then a wartime member of the Danish Resistance. He was captured and began the long years of internment, from which he emerged a little leaner but with his zest for life intact. His huge energy was now centred on the job in hand and enthusing over all things Indian. He and his family remained lifelong friends. Then the Scandinavian presence was further enhanced by the arrival of the first WHO BCG Vaccination Team, headed by a young Danish doctor who later became Director General of WHO. Their skills in administering what was then a very new discovery in preventive vaccine while training Indian counterparts saw the beginnings of the Tuberculosis Control campaign. Their spontaneous goodwill was infectious and life had an extra sparkle. And Diwali was coming.

Diwali, the Hindu Festival of Light, was celebrated with little mustard oil lamps in every window and lighting every path, and then fireworks far into the night, which the children loved. In 1952 it coincided with our long hoped for move into a government-owned apartment, now officially allocated for us to rent. This had its own kitchen, large lounge with dining area, two bedrooms, and two bathrooms with wash basins and showers, and a large hole in the corner of the stone floor for the water to drain away. No baths, but two tin tubs, filled by boiling up bath water in a metal drum outside over a sort of charcoal brazier. The apartment was on the second floor of a four-storey three-sided block which overlooked an open grassy space leading to the main road. Our corner was the side where the morning sun followed the length of the outside balcony throughout the day. The balcony widened into a patio with lots of sitting-space and I had wild dreams of lounging chairs under shady umbrellas, fringed by potted palm and window boxes brimming with flowering bougainvillaea. It seemed too good to be true.

We soon came down to earth. On the appointed moving day Alan disappeared, office-bound, and I made my way to our new home. The front door was wide open. Peering through the dust I could discern a small heap of heavily paint-splashed furniture, evidently our first delivery of hired Public Works Department standard household pack ('tenants for the use of') among the debris, ash and wood shavings and what looked like a stray component part of a ceiling fan. Glancing up, I noticed what seemed to be a two-bladed fan was indeed limping drunkenly and stirring up the dust. Then a genie with a broom appeared. '*Punkah,*' he beamed, pointing ceilingwards.

He turned out to be the official resident sweeper, due to clean up yesterday. I gathered he had been delayed by other duties. As I watched, speechless, he spotted a cluster of oily rags abandoned in a corner, then slowly and carefully swept them behind the refrigerator left by arrangement with the previous tenant. I retreated and made a furious start on cleaning the bedroom. Salvation arrived some hours later with Sukhlal in the office Chevrolet, who took in the situation at a glance. Excuses were ignored and the sweeper was reduced, quivering, to serious floor-space clearing. The lopsided *punkah* was brought strongly to the attention of the management and a new one promised. An assistant sweeper, armed with scrubber and a bucket of water and disinfectant, was borrowed from somewhere. Sukhlal tactfully suggested that I should return with him to the office for a lunchtime break with the sahib, away from the scene of operations. His fierce handlebar moustache and flashing eyes having imposed due order, the quiet dignity returned. I joined him gratefully.

Arrangements had been finalised with the Delhi Municipal Authority the day before to have the electricity reconnected, so we arrived that afternoon, with our small pile of personal possessions, to a spotless floor. We dusted and positioned our two borrowed *charpoys* (beds), one table and two chairs, and decided it was time for tea. The kitchen *chula* (cooking stove) was not yet functioning, so we switched on the one electric ring and plugged in the refrigerator. Neither worked. But we had some warm soda water, and the telephone was operational. Alan called the electricity authority, who explained that authorisation had been given for lights to be connected but not the power. That would have to be done after the Diwali holiday, which had now started. The sun was beginning to set, so we took the chairs and soda water out to the balcony and watched the magic of tiny lights beginning to gleam from all the homes around. It was at first like a glow-worm patchwork softly spreading, then growing in intensity as more and more lights appeared. When darkness fell, we switched on our bedside lamp as the first of the fireworks shot into a darkening sky. The whole of the city seemed to be glowing with light as the celebrations began in earnest, and our sole lamp suddenly turned itself off. We tried all the other light fittings without success. We began to feel like beings in the outer darkness when everyone else was in glorious light.

Alan managed to locate the telephone in the semi-gloom and we were assured help would be coming. Amazingly, it did. Light suddenly blazed from every room and there was a gentle tap at the front door. Outside stood a very small gentleman with appropriately Father-Christmas-type beard and very thick pebble glasses, clutching a large screwdriver in one hand and a handful of matchsticks in the other. He assured us he had replaced all the fuses. Alan followed him to the spider-web-encrusted fuse box down below in the stairwell. Father Christmas gave a farewell 'salaam' and departed on his way, with our profuse thanks and a very large Diwali gratuity. We sat beaming with delight over the soda water bottle to watch the last of the fireworks. Alan obviously had designs on the fuse-box matchsticks in the morning.

Exploring beyond the stair-well, I soon discovered the small nursery below the *gurdwara*, the Sikh temple at the back of Sujan Singh Park, with its abundance of exotic as well as familiar plants. There was jasmin, oleander, frangipani, and my favourite *rat ki rani*, or queen of the night, whose haunting fragrance hung on the air after dusk, cheek by jowl with marigolds and roses. Soon we had window boxes bulging with bougainvillaea, pansies and Livingstone daisies. Our screen of greenery then included a small pine tree in a tub for Christmas and a baby bamboo, which flourishes to this day as a bamboo grove in a Delhi garden. Almost anything grows in India if it has water, and the balcony tended to get muddy as well as being an oasis of greenery and flowers.

When we first met Ram Sarup, he was living with his wife and small family on the open ground between the apartments and the *gurdwara*. He was a very small man but, as we discovered later, he had the heart of a lion. He scrubbed floors until they shone, mopped the balcony free of every trace of my gardening mess, and boiled up bathwater when needed. There seemed nothing he was not willing to try, even to cleaning saucepans after my cooking efforts, which would never be even remotely envisaged in a strictly Hindu household. When the rainy season started, we moved him and his family into our unused garage. I think that is when the relationship of mutual trust was cemented. It too lasted over the years.

Many years later when we were posted away from Delhi we arranged with his consent for him to continue working for the new occupant of the apartment, and gave him a parting gift of some months' extra pay which he refused to take in cash because he said he would only spend it. When we offered to put it in the bank for him his horror was manifest ... he would never trust a bank. Then with help in interpretation from the ever helpful office accountant we reached a solution. Ram Sarup wanted us to give the money to Larsen Sahib for safe keeping, and when he needed it, he would tell him. So it was left.

Many moons later and many miles away, Alan received a letter from Poul Larsen. Ram Sarup had collected his money, plus interest because Poul had discreetly banked it. He was leaving Delhi to go back to his village. The next paragraph was brimming with Poul's familiar huge enthusiasm. 'Alan ... I believe environmental sanitation is catching on at last. Ram Sarup is using the money to construct a new well in his native village for his family and the other *harijans* (untouchables) of his community. Is that not splendid news?'

We all hope it still is.

7

Mustapha

The kitchen was a small dark hutch of a room, and for some reason at the far end of the long outside verandah. The *chula* was a large brick edifice with a flat top and four holes where you put the charcoal. The temperature control was a straw fan which, flapped briskly, whipped the glowing charcoal into flame and distributed hot ash and smuts impartially over the cook and the cooking. Emerging into blinding sunlight or monsoon deluge, depending on the season, was further complicated by the spring-loaded wire mesh door, which snapped briskly into action when you were halfway through clutching the meal. It was the accepted custom for 'proper' cooks to wedge the door permanently open to flies in the daytime and buzzing insects after dark. To be fair, this did cut down on breakages en route to the dining room. I resisted the temptation. But Alan was becoming unnerved by the shattering crashes or muttered curses as he rescued me from its vice-like grip. 'We must do something about getting a cook,' he said firmly.

I blinked away the sweat beads and looked at the mutton cutlets. Eyed dispassionately, they were not a happy sight. Undersized and spiky, they seemed to have shrunk in the cooking and huddled together on the dish, smelling distinctly of goat. 'It simply doesn't make sense to slave in the kitchen in this climate,' Alan continued reasonably. 'Besides, with Christmas coming, you will have other things to do.' He warmed to the subject. 'Proper cooks know where to get good meat. They've been doing it for years and have their own contacts. And they have a way with these stoves ... been using them for years and do marvels with them.' I began to picture the mouth-watering delicacies we were missing out on: juicy steaks, whisper-like soufflés, and that wonderful dessert decorated with spun sugar which every self-respecting Indian cook can produce at the drop of a hat. We let it be known we needed a cook.

The news spread rapidly. A steady trickle of applicants arrived at our door, mostly elderly with a forlorn and threadbare look, all with their chitties from previous satisfied employers. I did not know then there was a brisk trade in these testimonials, and of course it was fair game just to borrow them. So I carried on battling with the *chula*. Then Mustapha appeared. Resplendent in gleaming white uniform and towering starched head-dress anchored with red and gold braid, he exuded a certain dignity. With quiet confidence he mentioned he was accustomed to working only in diplomatic households. When I confessed our humbler status he was understanding. He had travelled far, he said, from his native birthplace in Lahore, now Pakistan, and had prepared his boily-roast chicken, spicy curry and caramelly custard in many fine homes. He was nevertheless prepared to serve us.

He started in great style. A small boy appeared from nowhere to scrub the kitchen. Our lack of essential kitchen equipment was pointed out firmly but quietly, so we hastened to remedy the deficiency. A small mountain of charcoal appeared on the outside verandah. Since this gave access to the whole length of the apartment including the bedrooms, the gritty particles clung persistently to the soles of our shoes and sprinkled everywhere we moved. But this seemed a small price to pay for domestic harmony. Meals appeared on time. No more spiky goat cutlets.

Every morning immediately after breakfast Mustapha presented his cook book and requested menu orders for the day. The cook book was a large ruled exercise book in which he recorded the items purchased and money expended the previous day. At first I found the entries confusing. My wits always have ground painfully into gear rather later in the day.

We can't all be 'morning people'. Mustapha was. I hesitated, puzzled, halfway down a column. 'Waggytables? Five rupees?' He repeated, firmly 'Waggytables. Five rupees.' Then, patiently, 'Carrots, v'spinach, onion...' 'Oh, vegetables,' I said hastily, trying to recall the two of us devouring the cornucopia of vegetables available in those days for five rupees. Mustapha read my thoughts. 'Two times yesterday soup.'

We seemed to be eating our way through vast quantities of butter, cream and bones too. The answer was always the same. Soup. He was obviously a connoisseur with greater knowledge than mine of the ingredients necessary for 'High Class Soup'. Alan was delighted with the regular appearance of edible food, and it seemed churlish to crunch through the barrier reef of charcoal to watch what he actually put in the soup. I suspected anyway that whatever he did, he did very early in the morning, because he always disappeared after the cook book session to reappear at meal times. But food always arrived, like magic, on time.

Christmas loomed closer and Alan was anxious about the turkey. 'Better get Mustapha to order it early,' he said. So we did that. Mustapha calmed our fears. He knew exactly what we wanted. With his contacts, the very highest class turkey would be procured and he would supervise the fattening and killing of it personally. The cook book accounts began to swell alarmingly. But now it wasn't just the soup. 'Mustapha, all that butter? And eggs and cream?' He shook his head sadly at the foolishness of the question. 'Turkey,' he said. 'Make fat.' I wondered where he kept the voracious bird but his answers were elusive. I imagined perhaps his diplomatic contacts included a private Cooks' Turkey Compound. But Christmas approached hotfoot and there were indeed other things to think about. Mustapha pursued his quiet way with the air of a man who has everything under control.

The great day arrived. The dinner table was set with care and lit with candles among the greenery. We waited greedily. First the soup. Then a long delay until Mustapha entered bearing aloft a large steaming platter. He placed it reverently on the table, bowed, and retreated. In the flickering candlelight we both peered at the tastefully arranged border of vegetables, in the centre of which crouched what might have been a very small chicken or perhaps an oversized pigeon. Alan reflectively wielded the carving knife. The emaciated bird resisted. He tried again. 'Can't cut the wretched thing. Good grief, it's like india rubber.' The vegetables were plentiful and we ate them thoughtfully. Serves us right, I thought, for gobbling all that cream and butter before it was even Christmas. Mustapha removed the platter and offending bird tenderly. Nobody said a word.

After the coffee, Mustapha reappeared unexpectedly, clad in an impeccable long white shawl draped over his uniform, a large rolled bundle under one arm. He wished us good fortune, smiled forgivingly, and bade us farewell. Was he going far? 'Lahore-side,' he said gravely. 'Urgent summons from diplomatic family.'

We never saw him again.

8

Septembers

Septembers could I suppose have been called our 'red letter' months. It was in September 1950 that Alan joined UNICEF in Bangkok, and September 1961 which saw our arrival in the different complexities of New York Headquarters after 11 years in India. Way into the future, September brought our first glimpse of Korea on a grey rainy day which gave no hint of the majesty of the mountains shining in December snow and sunlight, or of the red, thirsty summer sunsets when the Han River was almost dry after the long drought. And with September too came our first sight of the glowing beauty of Addis Ababa with the Mascal daisies in flower.

So it could have been no coincidence that our firstborn son timed his arrival for a golden Sunday morning in late September.

We were on home leave. Alan's parents, now retired, lived close to the rented apartment friends had found for us, not far from the old grey stone church in Prittlewell village so familiar from childhood days, when I attended the adjoining church primary school. It was a beautiful summer, with families and friends close, and Andrew was of course the loveliest baby, even if he stubbornly delayed entry into this world at the predicted time. But the christening service in St Mary's church, where I had been baptised and confirmed by the gnarled Australian vicar to whom I lost my heart at a very early age, finally went ahead as planned. So it was that we arrived at Southampton with a ten-day-old baby and far more luggage than usual, to sail for Bombay.

The gentle swell seemed to rock him to sleep. The cabin steward bent over backwards to help, even at bath time. The two weeks passed into a sort of hazy glow of a new kind of happiness which comes, I suppose, with the age-old miracle of new life in the birth of a baby. We arrived soon after sunrise, and I remembered that familiar smell, before the outlines of India Gate and the shoreline became clear, and we felt we were coming home.

Waiting at the dockside was the kindly Indian UNICEF local supplies officer, radiant with the good news that our long-awaited personal effects had at last arrived safely after many adventures along the way. However, one box awaited clearance ... hopefully the missing 'wooden box with padlock' enumerated on the original shipping list. We had almost forgotten our three small Chinese bamboo-pattern rugs. Somewhere along the line they had acquired the status of 'carpets' ... a word that seems to arouse unusual interest in Customs staff all over the world. Perhaps suspicion lest something sinister be concealed inside – who knows? Anyway, it took a very long time to settle, and even on a solitary bench in the shade, Bombay port can be uncomfortably humid. So by the time Alan and our good colleague returned I was running out of boiled water for a very thirsty small boy. Alan, with remarkable ingenuity (he was after all a very new father), located the engine driver as we were boarding the Bombay Express, and returned triumphantly with the baby bottles filled again with scalding water from the engine. True, they took a while to cool down. But it was a very long journey.

Amid the noise and confusion of Old Delhi railway station Sukhlal stood, calm and exuding dignity in his impeccably pressed khaki uniform until he saw the *chota sahib*, and the seriousness vanished in a huge grin and flood of greetings. All Indians love all babies, but boy babies are instantly treated like royalty and thrive on it. Andrew had a friend for life. Baggage was magically retrieved and stowed in the Chevrolet boot, safe transport fixed for newly Customs-cleared possessions, and we were whisked back to an apartment positively glowing with cleanliness and polish, vases full of fresh flowers, and the glimpse of the corner of a sari through the doorway as Sujata left us to settle in after her good deed in organising the welcome. Ram Sarup beamed with quiet satisfaction. It was indeed good to be home.

9

Mary

Mary was born in Darjeeling of Nepalese parents. She didn't know exactly when, and since she could neither read nor write there was really no way of finding out. Her life had been spent looking after other people's children. She called them the *babba log*, which translates roughly into the 'baby people', and she loved them with the fierce loyalty for which her Gurkha race are famous in the field of battle.

When our lives crossed, Mary was small and plump, her face walnut brown and smile-wrinkled, a clove tucked neatly into each pierced ear lobe, and she smelt sweet and wholesome with a faint whiff of spice like apple pie.

She did not apply for the job. I applied for Mary. She worked for the Counsellor of the German Embassy in Delhi, looking after their young son, who had now outgrown *ayahs* and was to be prepared by a German governess for school in his motherland. Before that, she was employed by a Norwegian Embassy family now serving in another part of the world. Long after Mary became part of our household, I had an unexpected call from the Norwegian Ambassador, who was passing through Delhi. He asked if he might call. He came for tea, not with me but with Mary.

Nevertheless, in those early days I had been warned about *ayahs*. They could be careless, lazy and none too clean. It was advisable to take a firm hand. So when Mary boiled up the first kettle of water for the baby's bottle, I carefully switched it back on again just to make sure steam was coming out. I heard a chuckle as Mary talked to our three-month-old son: 'Andrew, Mary has been *ayah* since she was sixteen years old. Now maybe sixty years? But your mother still thinks she doesn't know how to boil a kettle.' I could swear there was an answering chuckle from the cot. What is sure is that a mutual bond of trust had been established, and it never faded.

Mary made her presence felt. At 6 a.m. she was waiting, dainty in her pale blue sari, the cloves in her ears seasonally replaced by fresh jasmin flowers, to take the *babba sahib* for a stroll in his pram in nearby Lodhi Gardens while the morning air was still cool and fresh. The kitchen too took on an unnatural air of cleanliness, and we found Mary had been supervising the scrubbing soon after dawn. When the sweeper was suspected of having dysentery, the large bathroom bottle of Dettol was immediately purloined, and the cowering, afflicted little man made to disinfect his hands raw, and banned from *babba sahib*'s vicinity before we knew anything about it.

The dog was bathed, and the cat narrowly escaped.

The seasons in India passed swiftly in a succession of searing hot dry summers followed by shattering monsoon rains; spring when the jacaranda flowers were the colour or bluebells, and the Spring Festival of Holi was celebrated by dousing everyone with coloured water; autumn with Diwali, the Festival of Light, and tiny mustard lamps glowing in every window. And of course Christmas and Easter. Mary's child-like joy in them all was infectious. She disappeared about her own business only on Sundays, when she rang the bells for early service. We never knew where. We only knew that as surely as the morning sun rose, Mary would appear at six next morning, fresh and trim in her newly ironed sari, to organise morning tea and make sure the day started right.

10

Sitaram

Life settled into a pattern.

Three months gradually stretched into 11 years. The days melted into one another, the weeks into months and the months into years. A succession from gentle sunrise to molten sunset with the velvet night in between. Everything was slightly back to front, which was part of the charm. Spring heralded the blue showers of jacaranda blossom and the sullen scratching of dust storms as summer approached. Then the call of the brain fever bird as the mercury soared in the blistering noon sun and the Delhi Sikh taxi drivers were rumoured to be prone to brainstorms under the weight of the tightly wound turbans they wore proudly over long thick hair piled inside. Grass was seared and brown, and dogs panted in the shade. And suddenly the flame of the forest burst into a glory of deep orange blossom over the parched stony Ridge. The monsoon marked the beginning of autumn. Spring crocus came into flower, green mould sprouted on walls and ceilings and inside cupboards, and the air was thick and heavy. Then came glorious winters with thick white dew like frost on the grass in the early morning sunshine.

When I was pregnant I had evening sickness. The doctor nodded understandingly. 'That's India,' he said.

Shopping day was Friday, when I rattled into Connaught Circus, the heart of New Delhi, in one of the Sikh taxis from the rank by our local bazaar. I paid off the driver as we reached the defiant flybitten sign 'EMPORIUM', and went through the murky doorway of the Empire Stores. Inside, everything smelt of mothballs, with a faint overlay of insecticide. Shelves bulged with tallow candles rubbing sides with tins of slightly rancid imported butter; soda water, labelled confusingly cider water; open sacks of rice, sugar and flour heavily populated with weevils and 'the original' Roses Lime Juice.

Staggering out with my weekly haul of groceries, I always found a small boy waiting patiently outside to take the load. His name was Sitaram. He was perhaps seven years old and small for his age. His father peddled fruit, and Sitaram helped him, but did other useful things like 'minding' people's cars. In return for a small *backsheesh* he would make sure other small boys did not steal windscreen wipers or hub caps. He and I had few words in a common language, but we seemed to understand one another. And, as he said, he was 'my friend'.

He knew my next stop would be the vegetable market and pattered along behind. He made sure I was not cheated too badly, and doubtless extorted an anna or so from the vegetable man whose stall was chosen. The same thing happened at the bakery, and at the Pork Shop, which was the only place in Delhi where you could buy warm, damp bacon, freshly sliced. Sitaram then shot off with my mountain of shopping, to waylay a taxi. 'Honest driver, *Memsahib*,' he would say reassuringly. '*Sab thik hai* ... all will be well.' One last formality remained. Sitaram would shyly produce a small basket of his father's fruit from nowhere in particular. I would gently pinch my way round the apples or apricots or pears from Kulu Valley in season, extract a few of the least soggy, and produce my purse. Sitaram's dark eyes would brighten with triumph and embarrassment all at the same time. And then we both laughed. The rotting fruit became our shared secret.

When we left Delhi, Sitaram must have been 18, but he was still small for his age. We said goodbye formally, shaking hands. He held out his small basket of fruit. This time we did not laugh.

It was 20 years before we returned. We landed at Palam

airport for a brief visit at the end of June and stepped out on to the tarmac, into night air which felt like a warm bath. The monsoon rains were still approaching but the air was moist under heavy cloud cover. Next day the sun was as fierce as we remembered it so we waited until the relative cool of early evening to revisit Connaught Circus. We strolled under the shaded colonnades remembering familiar shops, dodging the beggars who sprang out from the shadows calling '*Backsheesh, Sahib, Memsahib, Backsheesh.*' One cry was more persistent than the rest. A very small man followed, nimbly outrunning the others. '*Memsahib*, Sitaram ... Sitaram.'

I stopped dead in my tracks ... and there was Sitaram. He had the wisp of a moustache, the same huge dark eyes, and he carried a small basket of fruit. To the utter amazement of the now swelling crowd of beggars and passers-by, we hugged each other. I said, 'Sitaram, you still selling fruit?' '*Aji* ... Yes,' he said. I pinched the shrivelled apricots very gently, and then we both burst out laughing.

11

The Maldives

In the early hours of January 9, 1955, five of the northern atolls of the Maldive islands were hit by a cyclone.

News did not reach Malé, the capital, for nearly a week. The Sultanate of the Maldives was defined by a distinguished Maldivian writer as 'what appears to be a splutter of the cartographer's pen in the Indian Ocean west of Ceylon on the map of Asia'. An archipelago of over 2,000 islands, it stretches some 470 miles across an ocean subject to heavy seas, strong currents, and away from regular shipping lanes. Links with Britain date back to 1887, when a State Agreement was signed by the British Governor General of Ceylon and the Sultan of the Maldives. British warships made regular visits to Malé during the war years, British troops were stationed on Addu atoll, and the RAF established communications through a radio transmitter and receiver. It was through this ageing device that news of the cyclone reached Colombo and the rest of the world.

The response was international. The Red Cross Societies and the Ceylonese government were prompt in organising the donation of money and food. UNICEF headquarters promised a shipment of rice and help with distribution. The economy of the islands depended heavily on fishing and husbandry; there were few crops, but the trees provided shelter, and the wood and coir were used for boat building, rope weaving, and for export. The coconut palms provided juice for use as toddy, and for making jaggery, the sweet palm sugar. The shredded coconut flesh was eaten with rice. The screw pine provided fruit similar to pineapple, and bread fruit was cooked as a vegetable. Dried and smoked, the ever-abundant surplus fish in these waters was exported to Ceylon to pay for the rice which did not grow on the islands. With the loss of so many fishing boats and widespread destruction of trees, the situation could be disastrous, and urgent action was vital. UNICEF Delhi office was the nearest to the scene.

So it was that Alan was sent off on the rescue mission to deliver a hundred tons of rice to the islands. The Larsen and Davies family were at the airport with me to wish him God speed and assure him they would keep an eye on Andrew and me while he was away. Flying via Bombay, he was greeted on arrival in Colombo early the following morning by the WHO Program Officer, and learned more details of the islanders' situation from the Maldivian government representative in Colombo, and the British and American High Commissioner and Ambassador respectively. A small ship was chartered and scheduled to leave Colombo for Malé at the week's end, and by Sunday afternoon the bags of rice, together with a large quantity of cotton clothing donated by the Red Cross, were loaded on the SS *Effigyny*, all ready to set sail by sunset. The other passenger boarding was Hugh Gibb, the *Sunday Times* correspondent, whose assignment was to photograph the islands and report on the effects of the cyclone.

The *Effigyny* was a sturdy little craft laid down in Amble shipyard in 1924, and still sailing the Persian Gulf and the Malabar Coast with a crew from Bombay and southern India. The master, Captain Ottley from Sussex, had been at sea since the age of 14. He knew the waters of the Malabar Coast as intimately as the Seven Sisters, and had carried all manner of cargoes, traversing the Persian Gulf, and the Indian Ocean, as far as the Maldives. Her two passengers duly boarded with their borrowed camp beds for sleeping on deck where it was cooler, and it became evident that the latest cargo had been goats and dried fish.

Her departure was marked by a prolonged agonised blast on the whistle which had become entangled in a loose derrick. Then to the amusement of passengers crowding the decks of a cruise liner in Colombo harbour, and the irritation of the pilot, the anchor refused to budge. It had become entangled in a mass of cables, buoys and waste material left by a careless dredger. This problem overcome and the whistle silenced, the *Effigyny* sailed off at sunset on a three-day journey across a totally empty and rather angry sea.

Having successfully braved the last narrow passage between reefs white with breakers, the *Effigyny* finally entered the lagoon of Malé atoll soon after dawn on the third day. She was met by the Sultan's ceremonial white barge with 20 oarsmen, who rowed the two passengers to the quayside where the Prime Minister was waiting to greet them and escort them to the Council Chamber for a briefing on the present situation. There were apparently two boats available for sailing to the afflicted atolls with the rice: an ageing motor boat called the *Hyacinth*, which was the only powered craft in the Maldives at that time, and a *dengi*, or sailing vessel, built of coconut wood and teak. The Prime Minister would be joining them on the voyage. The two craft were loaded with the supplies ready for distribution, but Captain Ottley had private reservations about the motor boat. The State Guest House was prepared for the visitors, who slept, in luxury after their camp beds on deck, under snow-white mosquito nets, having successfully discouraged the family of very large resident spiders among the folds ... I suspect Alan had his usual emergency insecticide with him.

When morning came, plans to sail off in the *Hyacinth* were abandoned as the engine broke down, so the little *Effigyny* bravely set off northward to Miladunmadulu atoll towing two laden boats in her wake. Anchored safely at last under the lee of Maladu island, the headman's rowing boat arrived to take his visitors across the lagoon to the eastern side and to the two nearby islands, which had suffered the full force of the invading sea. There the fisherfolk were already using the broken trees to mend the remaining boats. Many had been swept away, and the drinking wells were full of sand and debris, as was the narrow passage through the reef to the open sea. But the rice and clothing were doubly welcome.

The islands dipped below a glowing horizon as the *Effigyny* rolled gently eastwards. His passengers joined the captain around a rickety table at the stern. Between mouthfuls of Malabar curry so hot it brought tears to their eyes, they reflected on all they had seen, and wondered what the future would bring to these splashes on a cartographer's map.

12

Pearl Garden

The last time we moved house was, I think, in 1957. A ground-floor apartment became unexpectedly available in what were then the outskirts of New Delhi, on a corner plot and surrounded by a large garden. The blocks of two-storey flats were on quiet leafy side lanes adjoining the main highway to nearby Palam airport, and the new development was called appropriately Moti Bagh, which means in Hindi 'Pearl Garden'. We felt we had really stumbled on a pearl of great price. Our neighbours were mostly Indian Civil Servants and their families, and Andrew rapidly became inseparable from Ravi, the three-year-old next door whose mother taught at the local Catholic convent. So the home was run on strictly Hindu precepts during the daytime by grandmother, who welcomed the new friend as long as his shoes were removed before entry. Smokey the dog was discouraged.

Mary rapidly made herself comfortable in the servant's quarter at the back, conveniently close to a curry tree and the flowering profusion of what turned out to be a lime tree. Ram Sarup and family moved into the garage. The front garden had been used as a short cut for a herdsman with his cows, and what little grass was left of the lawn was dry and withered because the water hydrant had been disconnected. So a Sikh carpenter was engaged to erect a boundary fence of tough chicken wire, and the municipality in due course reconnected the water. Serious gardening could begin.

A visiting colleague from Bangkok brought some seeds of yellow oleander, and once the rat holes were filled and the dry earth by the fence dug and watered, we had the beginnings of a hedge, which grew into a flowering thicket. Water as always was precious. We had as before bathrooms with showers and our two portable bath tubs, and Ram Sarup would carefully carry the used bathwater to the thirsty new plants. I discovered that the *chaudhari*, the head gardener employed by the municipality, also ran a nearby nursery, so we rapidly became friends and exchanged treasures. By the advent of summer we had achieved a rose bed with generous donations from Sujata's garden, the transplanted bougainvillaea was a blaze of colour, the bamboo growing into a shield of green spears by the gate, and the little pine tree, still in its earthenware tub, thickening its branches for Christmas. With the monsoon rains the grass took heart and thickened into a lush green lawn, and the scent of jasmin and *rat ki rani* blossom hung on the damp air. With the spring came the magic of the new jacaranda tree in full blossom. But that was not the only surprise.

Nicky chose the first day of Holi for his precipitate arrival into the world. It was a national holiday to celebrate the arrival of spring, when adults anointed friends and passers-by with dabs of coloured powder, and enthusiastic youngsters showered everyone with coloured water from Holi sprays. The children just enjoyed soaking themselves and anyone crossing their path. Everyone wore their oldest clothes and joined in the fun. Alan, after a brief word by telephone with the doctor, revved up the little Austin with an air of grim desperation as we set off for the nursing home miles away on the other side of the Ridge. It was quite an eventful journey. 'Little Brother' was delivered safely on March 7, 1958 in Dr Talwar's Nursing Home.

Alan visited daily, and the doctor was kind and fatherly. He assured me the baby would soon put on weight and asked what we were going to call him. I said I was waiting for him to look like something. He said, 'Take it from me. He is one of those babies that doesn't look like anything until you give him a name. Why not name him David after me?' So we did that. He was baptised Nicholas David Angus in St James's church by the Kashmir Gate on what turned out to be the hottest day in May.

There is a magic about Christmas anywhere, at any age. But somehow it belongs especially to children. Perhaps that is why as life goes on, one remembers most vividly those Christmases when the children were young. The days of childhood are like the 12 days of Christmas: fleeting and infinitely precious.

In India, Christmas preparations began with shopping in the street markets of Old Delhi. Behind the Jumna Masjid mosque, there was a smell of charcoal, cow dung and open drains. But above all and pervading all was the dust. Bare feet shuffled in it, goats and horses scattered it with their hooves, bullock carts gouged it under their wooden wheels, and children played in it. It scratched your eyes, dried your nose and gritted in your teeth. It tasted slightly of pepper. Its smell was the smell of India, and I still miss it.

The streets were narrow, and a confusion of colour and noise. The shops were tiny recesses in battered stucco walls rather like cells in a beehive. They overspilled into roadside stalls, and between them impatient cyclists jangled their bells, shoppers jostled, and dogs, cows and goats foraged in the gutter or just slept in the sun. We threaded our way past the cloth merchants through trailing lengths of cottons and glowing silks, and found the toys. There were animals hand-painted in sandalwood, and clay birds in bright blues, greens and yellows. Glass bracelets were sold by the dozen, fragile as spun sugar and in every colour of the rainbow. There were balloons, rubber balls, plastic hoops, cloth dolls, wooden trains and marbles. There were always so many children in India who had so little that a gaily wrapped package from the Christmas tree would be clutched wonderingly as a fragment of a star fallen unexpectedly into small brown hands. We couldn't bring the stardust to them all. But we could make sure nobody went away from the office party empty-handed.

Sujata and I clutched our spoils, dodging the important

clanging tram hurtling down the middle of the street. It was overflowing with passengers clinging to its doors, windows and roof, the luckier ones jammed inside in cheerful confusion. It slowed down only for the old Brahminy bull, for whom everyone made way respectfully. A massive animal, with the distinctive hump of his breed and a dignity befitting his caste, he moved slowly, pausing every now and then to savour a mouthful of sugar cane, straw basket, or somebody's matting roof on his way to the sunlit temple courtyard.

From blinding sunlight into canvas-stippled shade, and we were in the street of the woollen merchants. They sold bright sweaters and scarves and socks and gloves for the chilly December nights, and we left with arms bulging with brittle-thin brown paper parcels tied carefully with string. We went past the street of the goldsmiths, where the damp shade glittered with the shimmer of bracelets and necklaces and filagree earrings. The merchants sat cross-legged behind small scales because their treasures were sold by weight. Bargaining was unhurried and enjoyed over glasses of sweet Indian tea. But we were bound for the fruit alley. Here the pungent smell of guava lurked between the mounds of Kulu apples and hard brown pears, as we sidestepped discarded banana skins and rotted leaves to buy brown Kashmir walnuts and almonds for the pudding. A leper held out the stumps of his hands by the water hydrant. Our shopkeeper poured him a drink.

Home again, I found the children immersed in the happy, messy task of dipping small balls of blotting paper into red ink to make substitute holly berries for the pile of green clippings to decorate the room. I hugged them, suddenly and shamefully grateful for having two hands and two arms. And two small sons. The cat took a leap at a trailing loop of crepe paper, wound herself furiously into a red and green cocoon, then just as suddenly froze into stillness to eye a dangling silver ball through the shredded loops.

One year the boys painted huge pine cones gathered in late summer in Ranikhet in the Himalayan foothills. They decorated them with loving care and a great deal of green, gold and silver paint. We still treasure the pine cones, but miss the small sticky fingers.

Christmas Eve, and the sun finally melted into the tawny clouds of early evening. Very softly, the familiar sound of a wooden flute hung in the air as a boy took his goats home. It was time to light the log fire and decorate the tree. In the firelight our resident lizard scuttled behind a picture frame, puzzled by the paper streamers trailing down his wall. When two sleepy boys pattered reluctantly to bed, each carried the largest pillow case he could find, and each determined to stay awake to listen for sleigh bells in the Indian night.

December mornings in Delhi are glorious. Crisp and bright with a sprinkling of heavy dew on the winter-green grass. Mary the *ayah* had her own views about most things, like spinach being good for the *babba-log* and dogs staying outside bedrooms, even at Christmas time. She dumped a tray of steaming tea on our bedside table and beamed 'Merry Christmas' before going about her duties of ringing the bells for early service. The dog whimpered and hid under the bed. The boys exploded from their bedroom with her presents, hugged her, attacked their own presents, and were soon excitedly ankle-deep in ribbons and wrapping. The dog at their heels chewed the large red Christmas bow attached to his collar. The cat quietly finished the milk from the tea tray.

Then the door bell rang with the first of a stream of well-wishers armed with the inevitable garland of marigolds. They presented their seasonal greetings and accepted their just rewards. There were the postmen, the flower seller, the vegetable man, the paper boy and the telegram boys. One year for no particular reason the Express telegram boys came. Alan at this point was trying to shave through a high collar of marigold petals which would have done justice to a giraffe. Marigolds anywhere have a particularly pungent smell and it mixed unhappily with shaving soap. And still the door bell kept ringing.

Breakfast with the Christmas tree lights winking and small nosegays at every plate, mostly marigolds. One from the *mali* who helped in the garden, one from Ram Sarup the sweeper, and one from Mull Chand, who was the current 'cook-bearer'. We never did achieve a 'proper' cook. But Mull Chand was well-meaning and a distant cousin of Sukhlal the office driver, who was in turn related by marriage to Mary's husband. The web of Indian family connections is bewildering, but once you are involved there is no escape even if you wanted to. Meanwhile there was the pudding to boil, the turkey to put into the tin oven for roasting, and of course the brandy butter to be beaten before morning service in the hush of the old Mutiny church on Delhi's historic Ridge.

In the churchyard the irreligious crows conversed loudly on the crooked gravestones. Inside, the morning sunlight softened as it crept through stained-glass windows. Altar candles stirred to flicker quietly and we knelt to remember the Child of Bethlehem.

I became less firmly attached to my little typewriter as the garden flourished, and we went through the joys of watching our two sons grow, and the anxieties of sudden sickness – dysentery, pneumonia, and, almost worse, 'fever of unknown origin'. We were lucky in having a sympathetic Punjabi family doctor, and a Bengali friend who was a paediatrician with daughters the same age as our two boys, and their support and help were invaluable. They were our only visitors when Andrew contracted diphtheria towards the end of our time in Delhi, and without them I could not have nursed him at home.

We also had the joy of watching projects we had seen initiated grow to fruition.

On early visits to the hill stations we had driven through the Terai when it was a steamy, malarious region between the Ganges plain and the Himalayan foothills. It was almost empty of people because of the dreaded sickness, so the land lay fallow because it was no longer tilled to grow food crops. It became a fertile farming area again with the destruction of the anopheles mosquito lavae in a joint malaria control programme, largely due to the boundless energy and skill of the

Greek WHO doctor heading the team. We saw the DDT plant joint project just outside Delhi from its beginnings when the foundation stones were laid. The women labourers in their colourful skirts and headscarves carried cement and stone up the rickety bamboo ladders in home-woven baskets balanced on their heads, with all the natural grace of Rajasthani dancers. Below, their children played in the dust with stones. The babies lay wrapped in pieces of cloth as they slept until feeding time, watched over by their 'big sisters' of five years or so. Completed, the plant provided DDT not only for local consumption but also for export. The penicillin plant in Pimpri, near Poona, was equally successful. The milk distribution schemes and sterilisation plant too are testimony to the dedicated staff who helped to achieve them, and to the enthusiasm of the Indian officials who worked with them.

But I think the lasting impression of those early UNICEF days 'in the field' was of being part of a family of varying nationalities but shared hopes and fears. In a way I suppose we were pioneers. But we were in good company.

Living so close to the airport, we were in the front line for arrivals and departures, and it was always good to see old friends on assignments from headquarters and further afield. The planes in those days were prone to rather uncertain timing, especially late in the day and in pre-monsoon turbulence, so many a departure on home leave or to fresh fields would entail an impromptu party in our garden while we waited for news from the control tower. Our colleagues in the WHO office hailed from countries as far apart as Ireland and Scandinavia, Israel and Czechoslovakia, Holland, Austria, Finland and Canada, so delayed departures were always a cause for celebration until the the dash to Palam airport. And of course the children enjoyed the belated bedtimes. Then there were the VIP visitors, for whom arrivals and departures were more formal. Danny Kaye was one of the first UNICEF 'Goodwill Ambassadors' who, having been 'officially' welcomed, proceeded to make an immediate hit with the children.

One of his first engagements was to visit the Najafgarh

Cricket, Lodhi tombs in background, India

Republic Day parade, India

Lodhi gardens, India

Maldives after typhoon

Lodhi gardens, squirrel-hunting, India

Holi spring festival, India

Naga children, India

Float-sharing, Hawaii

Oryx with crumpled horn, Awash National Park, Ethiopia

Woodland Path, Korea

Village Market, Korea

Yongsan Cub Scouts: Saluting flag, Korea

Red Sox little league taking the field: Yongsan, Korea

Village Elder
Korea

Harvesting Ginseng, Korea

Tammy's first born kittens, Korea

Winter, Han river bridge, Seoul, Korea

village project on the outskirts of Delhi, where a makeshift camp in the early days following partition had arisen when refugees from the north had fled the new Pakistan ... just as the Muslim refugees had fled in the opposite direction, with tragic consequences on both sides. Largely due to the selfless dedication of a handful of voluntary helpers including my paediatrician friend and her husband, who had been one of Mahatma Gandhi's closest followers, it was now a prospering and self-supporting community, with its own school and health centre. The children gathered round and followed their visitor as if he were the original Pied Piper, and were rewarded with a spontaneous miming act in no language in particular which had them falling about laughing. It was a joyous day for everyone.

A more serious Aneurin Bevan was greeted by the Health Minister and senior government officials but found an instant rapport too with Glan as a fellow Welshman.

And then of course there was the memorable occasion when the British Everest mountaineering team returned to Delhi triumphant with their success in reaching the summit of the mountain sacred to the Nepalese which Mary still called Chomolungma. Timed as it was for the news to reach England on the occasion of the Queen's coronation, it was marked by a party in the British Embassy gardens on a very warm June evening when the receiving line was distinguished by Sir John Hunt, Edmund Hillary, Sherpa Tenzing and Mrs Tenzing, and their strikingly lovely daughter. So life was not without its moments of excitement.

Over the years we had acquired a springer spaniel. He was a present for Andrew's third birthday and the two were inseparable. Walks in Lodhi gardens now became squirrel hunts. Smokey never caught one but he never gave up trying. He learned how to swim by falling in one of the Maidan pools chasing baby frogs in the springtime, and never did learn not to chase crows. Ram Sarup had made himself custodian of dog meals, which he would place on the back verandah under the shade of the curry tree. One watching crow would dive and squawk insults, and when Smokey chased it, barking furiously, the rest would descend and gobble up his meal. So Ram Sarup kept guard with a crow flap until the dish was safely emptied by the rightful owner.

Smokey was joined by a little 'jungly' kitten called Mimi who subsequently produced jungly kittens of her own, and the boys took turns to protect the sun bird's nest on the front porch when the eggs were hatching. There were always birds in the garden to nest in the trees and the now dense oleander hedge with its yellow trumpet flowers. The jacaranda tree had grown to shade the front porch, the new frangipani spread leaves with clusters of creamy flowers, the neem tree produced sap that soothed prickly heat, and the lime tree had a bumper harvest of fruit delicious sprinkled on papaya. The year the Council *malis* went on strike, our *chaudari* friend arrived to cut the grass with the large mower pulled by a buffalo. He said he feared there might be snakes in long grass after the rains which would harm the *chota sahibs*. And the buffalo was not on strike.

This time we heard of our new posting well in advance. We were assigned to New York following our home leave, where Alan for his sins was to do a two-year stint as Chief of the Asia Desk, where he would be dealing with complaints from 'the field' instead of sending them. There followed another fury of packing and sorting and disposing, complicated by Mary rescuing discarded *babba-log* items she was sure they would need in a strange new home. We had no problem in finding a young English couple who needed her services with their family but she was still inconsolable. Ram Sarup was to stay on with our successor, and so were the curtains. Smokey was found a new home with a WHO nurse who doted on him. Mimi and progeny were welcomed by a friend with a very large garden.

The bamboo-pattern mats were labelled, this time very clearly, and most things would have to go into store again until we found an apartment ... apparently not an easy achievement in that legendary city of skyscrapers and the

Statue of Liberty – and, of course, cowboys and baseball and hot dogs. We still could not quite believe we were really going.

We moved for the last weeks to a guest house in central Delhi, where Nicky immediately went down with bacillary dysentery, which complicated life and the journey home. Our final departure was spectacular for genuine warmth of farewells, but none the less heart-tugging. As the plane lifted off over the now familiar patchwork of fields, figures on the tarmac were still waving until they shrank into pinpoint size. It was going to feel strange not coming back.

13

New York Remembered

During a blissful home leave spent largely exploring the beaches and the still unspoiled Kentish countryside while Nicky, having recovered from his tummy troubles, reverted to a normal English 'pink' colour, and Andrew discovered the small crabs and starfish under the chalky rocks, it was a welcome change to have medical problems reduced to 'normal' coughs and colds. The two of them delighted visiting grandparents with their rapidly developing skills, Andrew with handling cricket and rugger balls, and Nicky with verbal repartee. Then my father was suddenly hospitalised with cancer. So Alan travelled as scheduled, hopefully to locate an apartment by the time we arrived. As the Thanet autumn gales heralded the approach of winter, thankfully my dad's treatment was successful and he rapidly returned to his usual robust health. Our goodbyes said again, the inventory rechecked and keys of the little rented home returned, the boys and I finally set off for the USA in mid-September 1961.

At the crowded Idlewild airport, no-one seemed to be hurrying. From the avalanche of baggage the right cases appeared as if by magic. We found the source of those do-it-yourself trolleys everyone else seemed to be pushing – no eager baggage handlers waiting to be of service – and emerged safely from the brusque Customs scrutiny to the outside world. The drive into New York City was terrifying. An unending stream of dark monsters with brilliant headlights seemed to be hurling themselves straight at us. The taxi driver was talkative, with the unnerving habit of turning round to make a point.

But nothing hit us. We came to know taxi drivers quite well, and they nearly all talked a lot. Except the one who picked up Nicky and me one bitterly cold snowy day and ran into the law. It seemed we were breaking the speed limit. A police limousine swerved in front of us, sirens screeching and lights flashing. It stopped. The law beckoned wordlessly to our driver. He stepped out wordlessly too and crunched off into the snow. We were left parked by the roadside, feeling very alone in that whirling white world. Nicky's lips quivered. TV crime movies had already had their effect. 'Mum, is he going to shoot him ... now?'

We were to live in Parkway Village, where Alan had miraculously found a furnished apartment, with the help of a friend who was another old China hand and lived there too. Located in the busy Queens district of New York, it was a triangular enclave between three motorways, and a haven of green. It consisted of tree-lined streets with generous grass verges and a very strict speed limit for any cars creeping through. The quietness was unexpected, that is until the children came out of school. There was a branch of the UN International School in Manhattan just at the end of the 'village' and well within walking distance. Most of the inhabitants were UN families like ourselves. The housing consisted of two-storey, split-level apartments with surrounding communal lawns and individual flower beds. There was a basement laundry with washing and drying machines for each block, but it was some time before I plucked up courage to investigate what the machines actually did.

The apartment was simply furnished and welcoming. The boys had an enormous bedroom upstairs overlooking the back lawns, and ours, smaller, was in the front. Uncarpeted wooden floors and stairs were practical if noisy and the kitchen was small but adequate. The boys had their first glimpse of a TV set with a bewildering choice of 13 channels. Alan disappeared each morning in his newly acquired Volkswagen Beetle, bound for the office in Manhattan, Andrew walked to school, and I discovered adjoining the playing fields a fiercely busy little side street leading to

Hellers the butchers, where I began to learn about American meat. To start with, the names were confusing. In India the choice had been simple: scrawny chicken, lamb that tasted of goat, and, of dubious origin, beef. Vague memories of English butchers with their tidy racks of lamb chops, Sunday roasts and rump steaks did not help. But Mr Heller did. I learned that mince was called ground round, there were T-bone and porterhouse steaks, and a pork joint I had never encountered before called spare ribs. This I discovered needed marinating in honey and soya sauce and broiling, which meant grilling, and together with hamburgers made at home with his ground round formed a popular part of local diet. His advice turned out to be sound as Andy's school friends started arriving at the door unexpectedly and it was a great help to have some 'burgers' stacked ready in the freezer. Nicky meanwhile divided his playing hours between two lots of 'best friends': the Japanese boy three doors down the street whose mother prepared sushi, and the Canadian twin girls next door, because, as he said, they had two bicycles and he had none. To his delight he was not allowed to go to school until he was six, and neither were they.

Christmas suddenly loomed on the horizon long before we expected it. Immediately after Thanksgiving, 'trimmings' and seasonal goodies appeared in the supermarkets. Our nearest was within easy walking distance and had been another revelation. I eventually grasped the difference between chilled and frozen food, and encountered undreamed-of luxuries like baked beans, canned hot dogs and paper plates. I planned to make mince pies for this very special Christmas and asked where I could find mincemeat. 'Butcher's counter,' said the young assistant helpfully. I tried to explain that in the UK we made pies at Christmas time filled with dried fruit mixed with brandy and suet. His eyes rolled in horror. 'Suet? Lady, you might. We don't.' I gave up on that one. The boys' excitement mounted as the toy stores displayed even more wonders, and ever plumper turkeys surfaced behind the butcher's counter.

Alan unexpectedly produced tickets for the opera. It was

Die Meistersinger, and the leading role of Hans Sachs was sung by Paul Schoeffler, an old friend from Vienna days when his wife Mary had been a colleague of Alan's in the IRO office and lived in the inn across the street from ours in Kindberg. I assured Alan I could find my way and meet him in Manhattan. With great daring I hired a baby-sitter, prepared the supper, settled the boys, who hardly noticed my departure, and walked to the local subway station. It started to snow. I counted the stops to the platform marked 'Lexington and 54th Street', and emerged to find two escalators going to the surface and picked the wrong one. No Alan. I battled through the icy wind and dazzling lights looking for the exit reached by the other escalator. It had to surface somewhere, But no. Perhaps it was gobbled up under the snow. I felt suddenly very alone in a hostile city. Then a policeman loomed up. He swung his night stick – what we call a truncheon. He looked down at me sternly. I said meekly, 'I'm lost.' He nodded as if this was not entirely unexpected. The other entrance was half a block away. He led me very carefully by the hand to the entrance on 54th Street and pointed to the escalator and said, 'Take care'. I did. The Opera House was warm and the music was wonderful.

Coming out, the snow had turned into a blizzard. The few taxis still on the streets carried little flags saying 'Off duty' and were wisely making for home. The city was very quiet. Suddenly a lighted cab. Miraculously, it stopped. Alan said breathlessly, 'Are you free?' A puzzled black face with very white eyes appeared through the front window. 'No, bud. There'll be a small charge.'

Back home it was warm and cosy and the garden was white under a brilliant moon. The baby-sitter thankfully took our taxi home. The boys were asleep. And Christmas was coming. I said, 'Shall we wake them? They've never seen snow.' So we did.

Christmas was wonderful. There were snowball fights and all the children built snowmen. There were carol parties and neighbourhood get-togethers and toys we had never dreamed of in the local store, although we did discover belatedly that they needed assembling once the packing was removed, which took us into the wee small hours on Christmas Eve. For Nicky, now nearly four years of age, the cardboard cartons were just as fascinating as the presents that came in them. So we really need not have bothered. Like all Christmases, it went too quickly.

The advantages of living in a 'developed' civilisation perhaps outweighed the disadvantages. I'm still not sure. It was difficult to quell the unease at seeing garbage bins loaded with cast-off Christmas trees complete with decorations which would have kept our *choudari*'s children happy for months. But life ran more smoothly with ice-cold homogenised milk delivered daily to the door, and a friendly milkman who once walked back two blocks through the rain to tell me to take my African violets in from the front path. Rain was not good for them. He was right. But encounters with automatic ice-making machines and do-it-yourself laundries could be scary.

Entertaining a visiting Indian guest who was a strict vegetarian brought its own complications. I knew he could eat only the middle cut from a certain fish and asked Alan to pick it up on his way home. He found it filleted before he could say 'Jack Robinson'. Conscience-stricken by my warning to be sure to bring it home with head and tail intact, he humbly asked the fishmonger to produce them ... one of his wife's strange habits, he explained. The vendor took one look at the impatient queue of customers, another at my husband. He then produced a barrel of heads, tails and bones, said 'Take your pick, bud,' and proceeded to the next customer.

Sudhir, our guest, was in New York as one of the delegation when Krishna Menon made his famously long, impassioned speech on the Kashmir issue to the General Assembly. I became familiar with UN Headquarters during our two-year stay, but will always remember my first visit. The vast, beautiful building is on the banks of the East River. The gardens were bright that day with daffodils under dark green trees, and the air full of the smell of spring. There was a crowd of demonstrators at the bottom of the steps leading to Tudor

City Place on the street opposite, where the wall bore the stone-chiselled inscription 'And they shall beat their swords into plowshares, and their spears into pruning hooks; nation shall not lift up sword against nation, neither shall they learn war any more.' This was not a war, just a protest. I forget what the protest was about. Certainly nothing to do with Kashmir. But the crowd was orderly, and obviously felt deeply. Four sturdy New York policemen were standing quietly around; watchful, not unfriendly. The traffic hurtled past unconcerned. A small boat hooted on the East River. Beyond this reasonably quiet oasis was the hum and roar of a city going about its business. A small bird sang.

Memories remain of searing hot summers, the heat trapped by skyscrapers; ice-cold winters when steam rose from the pavement vents where the homeless, like our cardboard city, tried to keep warm; the suddenness of spring, and the glorious colours of the fall; and through them all the bustle of a great city with its violence and unconcern, its unexpected warmth and kindness. Perhaps it all adds up in some degree to every city. New York was just bigger.

As we left by sea for the last time, the extraordinary beauty of Manhattan's skyline fading on the horizon in an ethereal silhouette of tall white buildings under a blue sky and never far from blue water, we passed the Statue of Liberty. The wheeling seagulls followed us out into the great Atlantic.

14

Land of the Morning Calm

The Korean War between the North and the South, partitioned along the 38th Parallel in 1945, had ended in 1953, but in 1963 when we arrived, it was still an uneasy peace.

The ancient name for Korea, Chosun, means Land of the Morning Calm. To most Westerners this little peninsula lying roughly between Japan and China on the other side of the world brings memories now growing vague of old unhappy far-off things and a battle that nearly involved the whole world. Or further back in time but tragically real to those who survived but still remember, the brutality of the prisoner-of-war camps in World War Two, where the North Korean guards were reputed to be 'worse than the Japanese'. Having spent my married life being whisked precipitately to odd corners of the earth, perhaps I had lost any built-in prejudices, but I had heard that autumn in Korea was incredibly beautiful: a land of sparkling sunshine, red-gold leaves, and humpy mountains like those in ancient scrolls, dignified old men in spotless long white robes and *'papa-san'* (grandfather) hats, and beautiful women in colourful silks.

The boys and I hopefully left London airport in the golden glow of a perfect September morning and landed half a world away, on a grey airstrip sodden with rain under a sullen sky, feeling that familiar damp chill like a bleak London morning as we peered at the large, dripping sign 'Welcome to Seoul' and wondered whatever happened to those 10,000 miles in between.

The old gentlemen were there in the black straw, high-crowned hats tied under the chin, and their womenfolk in a swirl of voluminous, jewel-bright silks. But most numerous were the children. Rosy cheeks, darting black almond eyes, flying pigtails or stubbed crew cuts, they seemed to be everywhere. They were undaunted by the rain, the screech of jet engines, the unsmiling airport officials and the milling crowds, and as I found later, by everything else...

The Koreans love children, and seldom restrain them. Wherever one goes there are always crowds of them in the centre of the action. They all shout 'Hello' at strangers with splendid impartiality. They play with fiendish energy and utter unconcern for traffic, as we discovered on the way from the airport to our new home in Itaewon. Toddlers, lovingly fingering the piles of stones at the roadside in solemn, round-eyed concentration, would make a sudden dash to the opposite side of the road as cars, buses and racing jeeps swerved in precarious semi-circles round them. Most of them seemed to have charmed lives. They rewarded drivers behind the strident horns and screeching brakes with innocent beaming smiles. So it was a hair-raising journey. Mr Oh, the office driver, seemed to have grown accustomed to it. I never did.

When the weather grew colder activity seemed to accelerate, and with the snow frozen into sheets of ice in the bitter January winds, the favourite game was sledging. Two small feet would be planted firmly on a home-made skate board improvised from any available piece of wood, on which the intrepid youngster would charge straight at the slithering oncoming traffic. But that was a hazard yet to come.

We left Seoul City by the ancient East Gate with its maze of market alleys, on to the main highway leading past the American Army base and ROK (Republic of Korea) barracks complex towards the Itaewon Foreign Housing Area and UN Village. Past the main American residential area with school and playing fields, commissary, officers' quarters and clubs, a steep curling little road to the left on Namsan mountain led to our rented bungalow in Itaewon, clinging to the third bend. There had been a landslide after heavy rain the night before, which had swept away some of the small Korean houses on the far side, so the road was slippery. But our bungalow was still there, and we were warmly greeted by Mr Kang, the Housing Office manager, who was busy checking that all was well. He became a real friend over the years.

When we arrived Alan had already taken to Korea like the proverbial duck to water. To begin with, it was his first assignment in charge of a UNICEF 'field' office, and from the start a relationship of shared trust and commitment with the local staff was achieved. Koreans have a tremendous capacity for hard work, and an infectious enthusiasm when it is something they feel is worth doing. So new programmes including health education, rural development and nutrition were growing fast with the active support of the government ministers concerned and with the villagers whose welfare they affected. To the delight of Mr Oh, and of Mr Kim the Transport Officer, Alan shared their enthusiasm for regular car maintenance. And as the periodic office picnics proved, he also loved their Korean food. So it was a happy office.

Autumn was as beautiful as they said, once it stopped raining. Koreans are all enthusiastic picnickers, and since Seoul City is surrounded by wooded mountain slopes, Sunday outings for the family with junior tied securely to mother's back in a blanket knotted round her waist were a familiar part of the scene. Cooking pans and chopsticks were taken along too, and of course cans of locally made beer. The spicy smell of the favourite *bulgogi*, thinly spiced beef flavoured with ginger, garlic, soya sauce and sesame seeds, mingled with the smell of charcoal and wood smoke. Then there was always singing. Koreans have been blessed with beautiful voices and a natural love of music, and they believe in using them. Autumn and harvest time also brought in the loads of vegetables from the countryside to the city, and that great annual event of Korean household life, the *Kimchi* making. *Kimchi* was more than a pickle. It was the average family's source of vegetable protein during winter, when nothing would grow in the frozen ground. Made from chopped cabbage, turnips, onions and a sort of horse-radish, spiced with garlic and red pepper, it was preserved in enormous earthenware *kimchi* pots and buried in the ground to ferment. Most foreigners find the smell alarming. But no meal is complete without it. Alan was already addicted.

After *kimchi*-making time, winter came suddenly. In Seoul the flaming red sunsets over the Han River slipped early into blackness studded with the myriad stars that seemed so much closer in the crisp freezing night air. People went to bed early, and Korean homes with their curved tiled roofs were shuttered and barred against the night and snugly warmed inside by charcoal briquettes under the *ondal* floor. The whole family would retire with a heap of padded quilts, usually in the room used for eating and living in the daytime, and to the comfort of a blissfully warm floor. The warmest part of our house was at ceiling level, where the air heated by the huge and very noisy boiler, which literally gobbled up fuel by the gallon, was expelled through the air vents. This did not go unnoticed by the rats, who scuttled busily inside the warm roof cavity until morning.

Outside, the streets were very quiet. There was still a curfew at midnight, and it was then one suddenly remembered that a peace treaty had never been signed and North Korean guards were still patrolling the border north of the 38th Parallel under the same frosty stars.

The boys had been enrolled in the Seoul International School, situated in the American Army base at Yongsan, and they settled in very happily. The headmaster was an American educator and writer whose grandfather had arrived in Pusan in 1895, so as a child he had lived in the heart of the old traditional Korea and was familiar with the historical background and culture. He also knew and liked the people. School teaching methods were relaxed and project oriented, and the pupils were American, Korean and generally international. Burgers and hot dogs and pizzas seemed more interesting than school lunches at home, and there were always milk shakes and orange juice and ice cream. Nicky joined the Cub Scouts and disappeared on mysterious outdoor activities aided by supplies of peanut butter and jelly sandwiches.

Andrew rapidly developed skills as 'pitcher' for the Little League Red Sox baseball team in the autumn, and for ice skating on the frozen pond when winter came.

Snow came early, but the American Army school bus still managed to crawl its way up the Itaewon bends on all but the worst days when the icy curves shone through like polished glass. Then, delighted to escape lessons, the children skimmed over the slopes on their toboggans instead, padded against the cold in hooded anoraks and ear muffs, their faces visible only by their bright red cheeks and smoking breath.

Korea was a land of multiple religions. The oldest was said to be Shamanism, the belief that daily life in the visible world is affected by the invisible world of spirits, and especially in remote country areas the Shamans are still held in great respect for their healing and prophetic powers. Buddhism is thought to have arrived in the early fifth century, and the large number of beautiful temples and historic shrines throughout the country testify to its widespread faithful following. Buddha's birthday is celebrated as a national holiday throughout the Republic of Korea. Confucianism spread from China at about the same time, and Islam is said to have been introduced by Turkish soldiers serving with UN forces during the Korean War. Christianity came with the Catholic and Protestant missionaries in the eighteenth century. But everyone celebrated Christmas.

There was skating on the frozen lake of Duk Soo Palace in the heart of Seoul City. Hot chestnuts and corn on the cob were cooked on little charcoal braziers and sold for a few won, and were warming for the skaters' hands as well as their stomachs. Friends brought Yuletide gifts of flaming red poinsettia, and Korean chrysanthemums whose branches were trained into graceful showers of leaves starred with little golden flowers, grown in pots festooned with trailing ribbons. Propagation and care of plants, and the formal arrangement of cut flowers and leaves, were taken very seriously. There were strict rules in this art, as with brush painting with its stylised themes of the four seasons: plum blossom, peony, bamboo and chrysanthemum for spring, summer, autumn and winter. Both were more difficult than they looked, as I soon discovered.

Soon after Christmas we were lucky enough to inherit Manji. Our nearest neighbours, an elderly American officer and his wife, had a far more well-ordered household than we did, with a full-time uniformed chauffeur and a very pretty Korean maid who understood English and organised the housework. They had been very kind in offering me lifts to the base when Alan was away on field trips, and on one memorable winter evening, finding us huddled round the fire in blankets when the boiler fuel mysteriously ran out, insisted on bringing in their supply of electric heaters and chasing up the recalcitrant oil delivery service to make sure we didn't die of frostbite. 'We know you British are not used to our central heating. But that's no reason for those lovely children to freeze when neighbours are at hand to help. Now do you need more blankets?' Their posting had arrived earlier than expected and they needed a job for Manji. So she moved in. Being a true Korean, she adored all children. And of course they loved her too. So we had harmony around the house and I had time to go to brush painting class.

Spring came at last with catkins full of pollen and forsythia dazzling in the sunlight. A rat was found dead in the garden. We were invited to a picnic, which turned out to be a traditional Korean luncheon party in the hills fringing the golf course outside Seoul. The house was quite beautiful with its curved tile roof in peacock blues and greens cornered by fire-breathing painted dragons to protect the home. Entry was through sliding screen doors to polished wooden floors where cushions were arranged around the low table for eating cross-legged. Carved wooden chests inlaid with mother-of-pearl flanked the walls. We were welcomed with the customary courtesies, and with tiny glasses of *soju*, the Korean aperitif, before food was served. Each dish, exquisitely arranged and taste-blended, was of different colour and texture. Crisp flakes of seaweed sprinkled with sesame seed complemented the sweet shredded pork and fiery red peppers, the tiger prawns and mounds of fragrant rice. We were so busy with these delicacies that we did not notice the boys go missing. One minute they were playing silly chopstick games and eating heartily. By the time the sweet came they had vanished.

Our host was immediately concerned. 'I will just check,' he said. We joined him.

Across the courtyard from the kitchen side of the house was a path leading to outbuildings. One of them housed pigs, with a family of small pink piglets, and I felt a twinge of guilt over the shredded pork. Then there were chickens and geese. Right at the end was an enormous wooden kennel. Inside, their pedigree German shepherd bitch was busy suckling her puppies. Her mate crouched outside, hackles rising as we approached.

'I go first,' said our host. 'She can be very protective.' So could he, I thought silently as the male dog sat quietly, stiff-backed and very watchful. Our host finally reappeared with two small boys beaming and intact. They had just been making friends with the mother and stroking the puppies, they explained. Our friend shook his head in obvious relief, still trembling slightly. 'Phew ... velly dangelous,' he said. Rs and Ls tend to get mixed in translation during moments of stress, which can make for confusion. 'But OK now. Your boys like dogs too much.'

It had been a lovely day. We forgot about it as time hurried by, until some five weeks later I had a telephone call. It was Alan calling from the office. 'Guess what I have on my desk?' I couldn't. 'A cardboard box containing one German shepherd pup. A present for the boys. Can you cope if I bring him home?' We could. Somebody lent a basket. Manji borrowed a feeding bowl and water dish, and the boys found a blanket and some straw. When the six-week-old puppy arrived, it was like Christmas all over again. He was the loveliest puppy in the world. With his long-haired black coat tan streaked, he was more like a small fluffy bear. But with huge, trusting dark eyes. We called him Brutus.

He became the boys' constant companion. Put to bed in his basket, he always ended up in their bedroom, in one or other bed, it didn't seem to matter which. They loved him and shared him. When the school bus arrived at the stop down the road, he was there with them. When he could, he boarded the bus too.

Brutus grew into a handsome dog, but he was almost too gentle and those dark eyes were ever watchful. As if he knew something we didn't.

One summer evening Alan and the boys took Brutus for his customary walk up the winding paths over Namsan. He always kept close, and when they raced to catch a ball he was at their heels. Then he stumbled. My first hint of tragedy was a tear-stained younger son hurtling through the door. 'Mum,' he gasped through his sobs. 'Mum ... Brutus has fallen down and he can't get up.' Neighbours were kind and helpful. Brutus was rushed down to the American Army Veterinary Hospital. He was pronounced dead on arrival. They diagnosed heart-worm, an endemic local parasite.

We were all dazed that evening. We all cried. The boys were inconsolable. I sat alone on the verandah when they finally went to sleep and as the shadows moved I thought I saw a familiar shaggy shape, felt those dark eyes watching me and stretched out my hand. But it was only a trick of the moonlight.

It was Manji who first heard. WHO friends who lived right at the top of our hill had a cat called Priscilla who had unexpectedly produced kittens. Manji knew because her friend worked in the house next door. I was beginning to learn the local grapevine was every bit as all encompassing in Korea as it had been in India ... and Manji loved cats too. So Tammy arrived, a shy little creature with a hint of wild cat in her tufted ears and no apparent liking for the human race. But the boys were delighted, and Manji had company in her room at night. News of the loss of Brutus had reached the American base too. A kindly major mentioned his English setter to Alan over lunch. She was a fine hunting dog ... guessed our boys might like one of the puppies. So another cardboard box arrived.

This time the occupant was a lively, tousled small puppy, with the unmistakeable dark eyes and tawny coat of the golden Labrador who was obviously his father. We called him Rough. He had a huge appetite, boundless energy, and his natural habitat would have been a grouse moor. After the first small spat there was a wary truce between him and the cat. As he grew, he ate his way through doormats and the screen doors designed to keep out summer insects, hurled himself at family and friends in a frenzy of affection, and took to standing with his paws atop the low fence surrounding the small front garden. There he could survey his territory, warning off would-be intruders, without realising he could easily jump over the top. Until one day, by accident, he lost his balance while barking at his arch enemy the newspaper boy, who wisely took off at breakneck speed with Rough in hot pursuit. But mostly he loved people, especially small boys.

One chilly autumn evening Manji lit the fire in the living room before the boys ate supper. Alan and I were out for dinner. On our return we found the big armchair next to the fireplace fully occupied. Rough was curled up blissfully, with Tammy occupying the warm spot in the soft fold of his still pink puppy tummy. A new friendship had been forged.

Three years slid by before there were rumours of budget cutbacks which threatened to affect the International School, now becoming increasingly popular with non-American students. If numbers had to be reduced, it seemed fair to assume that American dependants would be given priority in continuing education in what was after all their school.

The curriculum did not include French, which in those days entered the timetable at first form in senior school in the UK. So it seemed to make sense for Andrew to learn some. The idea was not greeted with enthusiasm. Together with a neighbour, the UNDP Representative, whose daughter was of the same age, we discovered a remarkable French lady who was willing to give a few hours a week to their tuition. She was a nun from Alsace who had spent many years in Korea since her ordination without ever returning to her beloved homeland. Lessons were fixed for Saturday mornings, and we held our breath as they went well and Andrew became fascinated with French poetry and *'les disques du Père Duval'*. She had a quiet gift for inspiring her pupils and we were grateful, especially when the baseball season came round and one pupil's mind wandered to the Little League practice session that afternoon.

The first Little League baseball game was on Saturday May 21 and was a great success for the Red Sox, but by then the blow had fallen. The headmaster was kind and sympathetic, but the decision had been made by the authorities that the school could no longer accept non-American pupils over the age of 11. Andrew's twelfth birthday would be in September, so the beginning of summer vacation in early June would spell the end of his days in the International School. Mother Zeller was genuinely upset at the loss of her reluctant pupil. She made him a very special present. It was a red felt sock, rather like a large Santa Claus sock, beautifully fashioned and embroidered with the message *'Pour André aux chaussettes rouges'*. We asked her what we could bring back for her when we visited her country. She said just a tiny handful of soil from La Belle France.

We decided to make it a very special home leave. Alan was due to attend board meetings in New York towards the end of June, and since the mileage is roughly the same whichever way you fly halfway round the world, we were encouraged by an American naval officer friend to visit him in Hawaii. We flew via Tokyo on the afternoon of June 22, and landed in Honolulu at 9.15 a.m. of the same day after crossing the International Date Line. Our friend was at the airport to meet us and drive us to our hotel; he said he would pick us up for dinner at his home, and left us to change into swimsuits. The boys were naturally ecstatic. A smiling Hawaiian lifeguard found them junior size surfboards and swam with them, and they were away. Then there was a lilo for safe paddling in the shallow water. Waikiki beach was the original paradise of sun, golden sands and shading palms, with American-style fast food and sanitation. And in those days there were still some chalet-style hotels with gardens opening on the beach. Ours adjoined the 'rest and recreation' centre for American Army personnel and their families, who were welcoming and friendly too. Our five days' stay went all too quickly.

We flew to Philadelphia, where friend Nancy of Shanghai days and her American husband took us sightseeing, and then suggested the boys and I stayed on while Alan went to New York. They had a lovely home in the leafy suburb of Awbury Park, where Nicky was delighted to find their two young sons had bicycles. He still had none. So we stayed. Daughter Mei Mei seemed to enjoy mothering all four boys and keeping them in order. Nancy and I managed to catch up with some of the 16 years in between. But the highlight of our visit was definitely the freak rainstorm that first evening, before Alan's flight to New York, when a giant tree in the garden was struck by lightning. There was a tremendous bang, and a dramatic sheet of dazzling light as it crashed to the ground. I think the boys were a mite disappointed it didn't happen again. We caught the Greyhound bus to New York a week later. Then it was off to London on our way to the rest of our home leave in our now familiar little haven by the Kentish coast. And school in England in September.

15

Home

The rest of that home leave was a bit frantic. We visited possible schools, and managed to acquire a home of our own at last. It was of modern noddy-box type, but surrounded by an old garden, with the remains of a shrubbery and a huge ilex tree, perfect for climbing and bird-roosting, and a view of the sea. It came also with a very long-term mortgage and a tiny kitchen which was almost cupboardless. Andrew was unusually emotional as he bounded into the kitchen. 'Mum ... is this really *ours*? This is the happiest day of my life.' Nicky just jumped to swing from the door lintel, which came away in his hands. But it did indeed become a happy home. And the beach was only a few minutes away.

A neighbour appeared to offer Alan the use of his electric drill. Just across the road lived a retired army officer, now housemaster in the local public school, who, with his wife, became longtime friends. He told us that a new house had just been established between junior and senior at the college. Andrew passed the necessary test and was accepted to start as a day boy from the beginning of the autumn term. Nicky was found a place in a small prep school which conveniently operated a 'brake' to collect and return the small pupils. There followed a visit to the official outfitters, where the boys were reluctantly fitted with the uniform requirements printed on very long lists. We then bought the essential Cash's name tapes remembered by generations of mothers who sewed them on by hand.

There were local buses and shops nearby. The Indian driving licence issued after passing my test in Delhi was not valid and I had never driven in the UK anyway. But Alan found time to locate a second-hand Fiat 500, as well as drilling the book shelves into the wall and taking the boys for a memorable day at Farnborough Air Show, before returning to Seoul in August. I began driving lessons.

The instructor had been a police driving examiner; he was completely unflappable and a man of few words. He said, 'Your husband ever give you driving lessons?' I nodded. 'Husbands ... bless them. Without them I'd be without a job.' He then went on to state that any woman capable of running a house and rearing a family was more than capable of driving a car, 'And not to forget it.' That did wonders for my morale.

While the boys were at school there was plenty to keep me fully occupied. Odd things went wrong, as I suppose they do in all new houses. I learned how to bleed radiators, and at one point managed to get the plumber, the Gas Board representative and the boiler company man all in the house at the same time to try and solve the elusive 'blowback' problem with the central heating system. They finally came up with the solution. The tall pipe in the outside passageway where the seaborne gales funnelled was shortened, then lagged with a sort of metallic tape resembling Christmas silver foil. It looked strange but solved the problem.

In October a buff envelope dropped through the letter box. I opened it in disbelief. A printed form giving the date for my driving test, on October 10. So much for well-meaning friends who had advised me to apply early because there was always a long delay. Clutching at straws, I told myself the date might be lucky. The Double Tenth was celebrated in China as the anniversary of the Sun Yat Sen revolution and therefore auspicious. It did not help.

My instructor was reassuring. 'Don't worry. We'll manage. Mirror, signal, gear. That's all.' I overtook a cyclist with sudden daring as he looked at the date again. 'I know that examiner. He's always on duty Thursdays. Grunts all the time. It's only his asthma. Don't let that put you off.'

October 10 arrived all too soon. He picked me up in good time for the ordeal, and waved me good luck. His place in the front seat was taken by a large man who levered himself disapprovingly between gear lever and the door. 'Temporary driving licence?' I showed him. 'Right ... number of that Hillman parked just near the corner?' I squinted and read it carefully. No comment. 'Let's go.'

Trembling, I avoided his jacket overflowing the gear lever and we moved slowly forward. Then the grunting started. It was more of an ominous, wheezing rumble ending in a staccato explosion as though he was fighting for breath. He won. 'When I tap the dashboard, a child has stepped under the wheels.' I braked hastily. 'Not *now*.' The wheezing became irritable. Then came a movement of the tweed jacket and the tiniest of taps on metal. I glanced sideways to see if he really meant it. His face was expressionless. Despairingly I braked hard, thinking of that child undoubtedly mangled underneath the chassis. My passenger was unmoved. 'Start up again,' he said almost kindly, and I knew it was the end. The boys would be tactful but disappointed. The stigma of L plates would remain. But I was quite calm now. 'Pull in to the left of this hill and stop.' I did that. 'Now start again.' The start brought us to the intersection with a busy shopping street, and every vehicle in Thanet decided to rush past. I waited. Then a sudden space, and I crept forward to stop suddenly as the engine stalled. I hardly noticed the wheezing any more, just changed into neutral and started again.

The rest of the journey was uneventful. He took out his pad, cleared his throat, and said, 'I have pleasure in telling you that you have passed your test.' As he scribbled I heard myself saying, 'Are you sure?' He tore off the page and handed me the pass slip. 'People often stall engines,' he said. 'Depends what they do afterwards...'

Jubilantly I waved the precious slip at my waiting instructor. 'Told you so,' he said. 'Now move over,' I relinquished the wheel. He grinned wickedly. 'Been too close to death before with new lady drivers.'

This small triumph made life much easier. Andrew unexpectedly developed a sudden interest in ballroom dancing classes in the church hall, so I was able to ferry him back and forth to nearby St Peter's village. I suspected our neighbour's blonde daughter Sally might have had something to do with it when he invited her to join him and his favourite Uncle Bill for a visit to the Boat Show in London during the Christmas holidays. Otherwise his favourite new activities were tennis in the summer, rugger in the winter, and squash all the year found. I think he found cricket a bit slow after baseball. Nicky, conversely, when he was not reading, absorbed in home-kit model making, or busy working on innovations to the Scalextric cars and track, preferred hockey, where, as he said, you at least had a weapon.

It was lovely to have a home to welcome them to, and for the boys to catch up with their grandparents again when my mother and father came for Christmas. They formed an instant rapport with my father, who was always doing the Wrong Thing, like taking them for a walk on the cliffs and introducing them to slot machines at his favourite seaside 'local' when he suddenly got thirsty. But it was grandma who told them stories and made the best fudge.

Our new 'hometown' was a warm and supportive little community, and the boys soon collected friends. Weekends and holidays the house and garden tended to overflow with visiting boys. Some of the mothers became my friends and mostly still are, now in our grandmotherly years.

The following September Andrew became a 'senior' in the college and joined Lodge House, which meant becoming a boarder. The little Fiat did a sterling job loaded with the big steel trunk full of necessities duly marked with Cash's name tapes, books and sporting gear, and in those days bedding and blankets, as we drove over to the main college building. The quadrangle was a confusion of new boys, trunks which had to be manhandled up a flight of steps, and waiting mothers who tended to get in the way. Andrew immediately found a friend from his old house and waved goodbye cheerfully as they heaved the trunks between them. There didn't seem much point in hanging around, so I waved back. But it was always to be a horrible wrench parting.

Nicky and I rejoined Alan in Seoul, where we were welcomed by Rough with almost hysterical enthusiasm, and more discreetly by Tammy and Manji, when Alan fetched us from the airport. Nicky went back to the International School and renewed his Cub Scout activities. And I caught up with entertaining and Alan's social obligations. One of them must have been prophetic. We were invited to a reception at the Capitol Building honouring His Majesty Emperor Haile Selassie of Ethiopia. His slight and almost boyish stature was belied by the strong handshake, strikingly piercing blue eyes and immense dignity.

Our assignment in Korea stretched into seven years. Looking back, they were a confusing mixture, like a balancing act between two worlds. My problem was the distance between them.

In those days, international staff had home leave every two years. Children attending schools at home were entitled to travel to their parents' duty station for one of the three school holidays each year. Since Korea was about as far as one could be from UK, extra visits either way were financially out of the question. That tended to give a feeling of isolation when the family was separated. Nicky followed in his brother's footsteps two years later when he reached the ripe old age of 11 years. I stayed in England again for his first year as a day boy. Then he joined Andrew as a boarder in Lodge House. I missed them both.

For Alan, the continuing success in programmes, including health, rural development and nutrition, was echoed in the loyalty and dedication of the local staff in a happy office. I too had reason to be grateful to all of them for their kindness and support when help was needed, and for their friendship. Suki, Alan's secretary, invited us to her wedding. She still writes every Christmas. This year was no exception. Her younger son would be graduating in February. Her daughter now had a daughter of her own, and correspondence with her elder son and two grandsons living in the USA was by email ... a far cry from her old office typewriter.

Korea is long independent of UNICEF assistance, and the office, having completed its job, no longer needs the original local staff. But Suki says they still keep in touch. There was to be a UNICEF charity bazaar before Christmas, and all the old staff would be there.

It was good to be home again in 1970 in time for the beginning of the long summer school holidays and the inevitable end of term reports, Andrew was still leading the class in French and, rather to our surprise, 'becoming a very useful member of the school orchestra and improving in all the aspects of violin playing'. This must have been the beginnings of the later devotion to his guitar. Nicky was struggling with the clarinet but 'showing a commendably clear grasp of Maths and Physics'. We watched them both compete in the nearby Walmer Tennis Tournament, and rounded off summer revisiting Austria and then seeing the Passion Play at Oberammergau for the first time. Back in Kent, there was time to relax and enjoy home before even thinking about packing. This time we had word of our next assignment in good time.

It was Ethiopia. The boys would be able to join us for the Christmas holidays in the legendary 'Land of 13 months of sunshine'.

16

Ethiopia

In Amharic the word *ferenji* means 'foreigner', that is, anyone who is not Ethiopian. In twenty-five years of gypsying round the world as a 'U.N. wife' I had heard it in many languages. But with the perversity of life, never felt more instantly at home than when we set foot on the rain-soaked tarmac of Bole airport, Addis Ababa, both blinking like dormice in the blinding sunlight. It was 8.30 on the morning of 26 September 1970. We were perhaps lucky to have arrived in the old Ethiopia, to depart in the birth pangs of the new. I only know that the enchantment of Africa's 'Hidden Empire' and the inherent dignity of its people hit me hard, and the wound of parting still hurts.

But to begin at the beginning...

Our first glimpse of Ethiopia was bright yellow. Like mirrored sunshine. We were circling over the Old Airport area of Addis Ababa before landing on an airstrip hemmed in by fields knee deep in Mascal daisies. We stumbled towards the Health and Immigration section where officials in immaculate khaki uniforms waited. Coming from our proudly National Health oriented homeland, it was a relief to have the obligatory current cholera immunisation entries in our little yellow books duly stamped after careful inspection. That hurdle over, we recovered our heavy baggage with the assistance of a small army of baggage handlers, and approached Customs. A dignified and very alert young officer, once convinced we carried no guns, ammunition, or gold bars, welcomed us to his country with the traditional greeting *Tenastalign* ... or 'God be with you'. We were quite sure He was.

The road from the airport was a modern two-lane highway, the middle verge green with grass and shrubs. Traffic was quite fast, but the occasional countryman with his patient retinue of donkeys laden with packs twice their size wandered unscathed among racing Fiat taxis, bicycles, and a dignified procession of flag-bearing Embassy and Government cars.

Small boys played mysterious games perilously close to the kerbs. Traffic lights heralded the entry to a roundabout. On the left was the white marble edifice of the Italian Juventis Sports Club, and on the right a sloping meadow where preparations for a gigantic bonfire seemed to be in progress. A few hundred yards further on, we took a left turn round the jacaranda trees now comprising the middle lane, and turned into the driveway of the Ethiopia Hotel.

The Commissionaire was an imposing figure in uniform heavy with war medals and a smile displaying teeth reminiscent of Gibbs Ivory Castles. The subdued light of the foyer revealed leather armchairs and settees, potted plants, and a reception desk with travel brochures, postcards and colourful posters welcoming guests to the 'Land of thirteen months of sunshine'. A welcoming young manager had the hotel register at the ready. Still in that dream world of singing ears from the flight and the altitude, we unpacked the top layer of relatively uncrumpled clothes, discovered hot water did indeed come out of the shower nozzle, and ventured out towards the jacaranda trees and our first close encounter with Ethiopia's capital city.

Beyond the hotel doors was another world. Small boys selling postcards and coins, bigger boys with Ethiopian brass and silver crosses, and waxed scrolls depicting the Saints, and the legendary meeting of King Solomon and the Queen of Sheba. A leper with his bell, an old man carrying a basket of onions on his head, all vied for attention at the same time. A roundabout with a confusing system of double traffic lights led to a choice of roads. One to the Haile Selassie cinema and then past souvenir shops, hairdresser, butcher and grocery stores to the railway station with its Buffet de la Gare, and the other past the Commercial Bank of Ethiopia, and then half left to the pharmacy and the Jimma Road, or right up a very steep hill where Churchill Avenue led through a series of traffic lights past the main Post Office, the Duke of Harrar hospital, the Lycee Mariam school and Polymatardis Greek supermarket, to Banca da Roma and City Hall right at the top.

Traffic was bewildering. The Ethiopians drive with the same verve but sometimes less skill than the Italians. Their traffic police terrified me. They were all very large, clad in tight belted uniforms and formidable peaked helmets, fiercely ready to leap aboard their snarling motor bikes in pursuit of an errant motorist. I learned later that they were equally ready to hold up the entire city traffic to escort an aged grandmother and her grandchildren and accompanying livestock safely to the other side. Since it is a mere half century since the main city traffic moved on horseback, whereas grandmothers will always be around, this makes a lot of sense. The police undoubtedly had grandmothers too.

Back at the hotel we discovered our arrival had coincided with the Feast of Mascal which celebrated the finding of the True Cross ... I am still not sure when, but in Ethiopia time is different too. Christmas and Easter fall later than ours and Lent lasts for sixty days and sixty nights and the fast is scrupulously observed. History and legend are forever intertwined and faith is very strong. That night we heard the priests chanting and cymbals clashing as the flames leapt higher. The fierce glow of the bonfire lit the whole night sky and we fell asleep with the shrill ululating and hollow drum beats still throbbing in our ears. It was another world, another time. The magic never faded.

I loved everything about Addis Ababa. I loved the morning light over the eucalyptus groves bordering the Little Akaki River near our house, the dramatic red of sunset-massed clouds and then the sudden dark. The stars seemed very close. There were dim lights from the *tukuls* (simple round dwellings built of local wood) further down the road.

At the one nearest to our gate we knew the lady who sold home-brewed *tullah* – a very potent beer – would be shepherding her children and her calf safely indoors for the night. Then the packs of hyena would start roaming, and at their first eerie call the dogs would bark. Otherwise nights were very quiet.

We rented a house in the Old Airport area of Addis. Our landlord was a delightful, rotund gentleman of the Shoan tribe. We were invited for tea on his terrace and fell instantly in love with the garden. The lawn sloped away from the little house to a tall hedge starred with blue flowers of morning glory. The land beyond the hedge was hidden, but it led to a cluster of thatched *tukuls* and our Ethiopian neighbours, and then to the Little Akaki River. Rising from this small valley the hills were forested with eucalyptus all the way to Entoto. At sunset their leaves turned silver and pale trunks glowed in the brief splendour of the afterglow. There was never any twilight. Then the sky was close and velvet-dark until, as if switched on by an unseen hand, the stars glittered.

The house was built of grey stone, rough and reassuringly solid. The lounge-dining room had a wooden plank floor and scattered rugs. A huge grey stone fireplace occupied most of the far wall and was piled with eucalyptus logs which burst into flames at the flicker of a match. There was no other heating. Nights at 9,000 feet altitude were chill in September, but the fire warmed the whole house. There was a tiny kitchen with wooden shelves and cupboards, a sink, a refrigerator, and an Italian cooker which ran on Calor gas. I discovered later the cooker had a small electrically operated rotisserie hidden from immediate view, and a distinctly Italian temperament. There was one large bedroom, with windows overlooking the rose terrace. Heavy wooden shutters were lowered at nightfall to discourage intruders like hyenas and the beautiful tawny serval cat I spotted one evening much later on, pressing his nose against the glass doors of the lounge. One bath and one shower room. And a guest room with twin beds and its own patio opening on to the vegetable patch. Just inside the front door I discovered a tiny 'study', furnished with a desk, a chair and a day-bed covered in blue and green check cotton and looking out towards the Entoto hills. It was unbelievably peaceful and welcoming. This was home for the rest of our stay in Ethiopia.

Our landlord had his own unique way of collecting the rent. He would call us and ask for a convenient time. Then he wouldn't come. Some hours later, or sometimes after a day or so, he would arrive beaming with goodwill and patient of our strange foreign obsession with time. He would enquire after our health, bemoan the state of business and world affairs, and graciously accept a cup of tea or a glass of something stronger. Then he would bring us up to date with the doings of his business and his family. His wife was a doctor who worked very hard for very low pay. His daughter was studying at an American university which was costing them a great deal of money. That was the time for Alan to produce, discreetly, the sealed envelope. After that we all had another drink and he bade us farewell until next month. We came to look forward to his visits and learned a great deal about his country, its ways and its history. And I think he enjoyed coming.

We inherited the day and night *zabanyas*, Shumi and Mingestu. Shumi was the day watchman and one of nature's gentlemen. He spoke no English and I had but a smattering of Amharic, but the respect and acceptance were mutual. I never discovered what time Shumi arrived in the morning, but the kettle was always boiling for our morning tea. Alan's car was polished and shining and the gates swung open when it was time for him to leave for the office. Floors were polished, mats hung out in the sun, and bathrooms clean and tidy. Then Shumi would busy himself in the garden. Among the vegetables he grew a fine crop of red chile peppers to make *wot*, the fiery spice which is the basis for most Ethiopian cooking. He grew *gorma* too – a sort of bitter spinach. We tried it, and to Shumi's alarm enjoyed it, so he quietly increased the sowing and watering. He was never intrusive. Just quietly always there. I still miss him.

Mingestu, the night watchman, was made of even sterner

stuff. He would arrive just around sunset and prepare his mint tea in the kitchen. There was a patch of mint growing conveniently right outside the kitchen door, and I suppose we supplied the tea and sugar. Either way, it was obviously good for his health. And it helped him to sleep at night. I have no idea how old he was, but he was known respectfully as *ababa* which means 'grandfather', and always arrived on duty resplendent in a pith helmet and long army greatcoat breast-deep in rows of medals earned during the Italian war. He would salute smartly before disappearing to re-robe himself in layers of woollen shawls for his guard duty. Then he slept soundly until morning on a wooden stool propped up against the wall adjoining the lounge chimney where it was warm. On waking, he would always water the roses before leaving in the morning. The rainy season made no difference. He would still be out there with his hose.

We solved the question of night-watchfulness after our first and only burglary. We staggered into the kitchen in search of morning tea to find for once no boiling water, but an angry harangue outside as Shumi upbraided Mingestu for allowing *shiftas* to break into the garden outhouse and steal his broom and *mamouti* – a sort of all-purpose gardening tool like a cross between a pickaxe and a hoe. When the argument died down, a subdued Mingestu went off with great dignity in his pith helmet and greatcoat. And Shumi indicated he knew where we could acquire a watch-dog. The theory was that in case of intruders, the dog would bark. This would have the dual purpose of frightening off the intruders and of waking Mingestu.

That is how Simba came to join the household.

Shumi had heard of a family living a few miles away down the Jimma road whose pair of pedigree Alsatians had produced six puppies. They were offering them at a very reasonable price to good homes. So we obediently made contact with the owners and fixed a date to see the puppies.

It was a large, rather untidy compound. The mother dog and pups were in an outbuilding with straw-covered floor and we asked if she was an 'inside' or 'outside' watch-dog. The owners confirmed her 'outside' status. The father of the pups appeared to be away somewhere, but we were assured he too was a pedigree 'outside' Alsatian and suitably fierce. We looked at the wriggling little bodies, all wet noses and wagging tails, and of course we were lost. A price was mentioned and Shumi coughed discreetly and had words in Amharic with the owner. Negotiations were obviously going to take some time, so we played with the puppies and talked to the mother, who was gentle and trusting. She had a beautiful head, large dark eyes, and the alert ears of her breed. One puppy was plumper and more active than the others and kept making comical attempts to lunge through the straw into our arms and tripping over his short legs. His warm little tummy was round and pink. 'Probably worms,' said my husband thoughtfully.

Finally an agreement was reached over the price and we promised to pick up the puppy when he was six weeks old. Shumi was delighted. We bought a large wicker basket to allow for growing and Shumi produced some clean straw from somewhere. Then to his amazement we went shopping for a puppy harness and warm blanket. He indicated that Ethiopian dogs were accustomed to stout collars and chain from an early age. And a blanket? Shumi shrugged his shoulders in polite disbelief at the idiosyncrasies of the *ferengi* but did not interfere.

It was the week before Christmas when we brought the puppy home. The plump one. Our two sons had just arrived from England for the school holidays and thought he was the best Christmas present ever. They hugged him and played with him gently and christened him Simba, which is Amharic for lion, so he had early delusions of grandeur. He continued to trip over his short legs and looked bewildered when he bumped into objects instead of walking round them, and when encouraged to 'sit' would roll on his back and wave his paws like an overgrown wood-louse. 'Think he's mentally retarded?' said our elder son, who was interested in psychology. 'Oh no, he'll grow out of it...'

Grow he certainly did. Apart from his ears. They remained

floppy and indeterminate. In three months he had outgrown his harness and his basket, then chewed his way through his first adult collar. So we bought a stronger one. That lasted nearly a month. He seemed to need the reassurance of human company – perhaps missing his brothers and sisters as we missed our sons now back in England – so at night he slept just outside our bedroom door. But unless we locked it, he would ease his way in and wake Alan with heavy breathing on his pillow. He never tried my side. So we decided it was time to get him used to the idea that at night he was an 'outside' dog. He still bolted for cover at the first sound of a hyena or jackal in the distance. But when he discovered Mingestu sleeping outside the warm living room chimney wrapped under a blanket in which he secreted his supper of *injera* bread and was willing to share, Simba joined him and slept happily. So we had two sleeping watchers.

Quite early on he had a disastrous encounter with the large cat who belonged to our Ethiopian neighbours on the other side of the wall. He suddenly noticed her washing her paws unhurriedly in the sunlight of our vegetable patch, gave a yelp of surprise, and hurtled across the garden as she made a dignified ascent to the top of the wall. She casually finished her grooming, leant over as he made a flying leap, and caught his nose with her curved claws. Simba retreated bleeding and whimpering for comfort. After that he tended to keep his distance from the wall.

Relative peace made with the cat, he attacked other things, including any car entering the gate. He would bark horrendously, grinding his teeth on the hub caps. He became expert at opening bolts and door handles. He bit almost everything except me. But it certainly kept us free of unwelcome intruders as his reputation spread.

By this time we had resorted to a massive leather collar more suited to a horse, attached to another strong link chain between two metal poles to restrict his activities when unsupervised.

We had a party one evening. Things were going splendidly until a noise like the clanking chains of Marley's ghost approached the open front door. Simba appeared, in friendly mood since he could smell food, and guests scattered for cover. Shumi, diligent as ever, hastily passed Simba a sausage roll, took hold of the tattered remnants of the chain, and led him away.

Five minutes later, the terrified glance of an Indian guest drew our eyes to the door. 'Do you have *two* dogs?' he gasped wonderingly. We bought yet another chain the following morning.

The altitude of 9,000 feet tended to make foreigners breathless, so it was nice to get away from it all sometimes for a weekend.

We tried to leave at sunrise. Then the roads were emptier, the droves of cows and shoats (a cross between a sheep and a goat) still peaceably munching grass far from the roadside. There were no fences. We encountered the odd speeding truck, and inevitably a village dog bent on suicide, as the road wound gently downhill to the lower clime of Debre Zeit. There we had breakfast on the terrace of the hotel beside the crater lake. The tantalising smell of hot fresh bread, bacon and eggs, and wonderful strong Ethiopian coffee wafted from the kitchen while we watched the birds who nested in the acacia groves nearby. There were glimpses of the malachite kingfisher, its cobalt crest vivid among the dark bullrushes on the lake verge. Red-headed weaver birds were as numerous and active as our sparrows. If we were very lucky we would spot the trailing blue plumes of a paradise flycatcher. The Rift Valley is sanctuary to an abundance of native birds, but there is still room for the flocks of migrants from our European winters.

Back on the road beyond Nazareth, the next village, the scenery changed. We passed the familiar black lava crater overgrown with poison green leaves of creeper, and then the Fantalle hot springs with their palm trees and pools of turquoise blue hot bubbling water that smelt of sulphur. Driving lower into the Rift Valley, vegetation became limited to thorn bushes dotted with nests of weaver birds. The country grew wilder and more beautiful. Journey's end was the thatched entrance gate to the Awash National Park.

The gatekeeper was an old friend, but he still wrote out a careful receipt for our entrance fee of one Ethiopian dollar (about 30 pence) before letting us pass. We drove slowly down the bumpy track, trying to look everywhere at the same time. Our favourites appeared first. Two dik-diks turned enquiringly, all huge eyes and soft quivering ears. A flurry of tiny birds rose like a swarm of insects. And suddenly, there in a clearing was the oryx with one crumpled horn. We felt we were coming home.

Our little tent was pitched by the Awash River. Under the fierce sun there was always a breeze by the water. As we sat eating our picnic lunch, the leaves of a huge fig tree on the bank quivered. A twig snapped. We looked up to see a small vervet monkey nibbling a fig. He glared down. Then with a tremendous crashing of branches and lashing of tails, the whole tribe swung through the tree. The small monkey tossed away the remains of his fig, casually eyeing the bananas on our table. He crept down carefully as though quite uninterested, grimaced fiercely, then with a sudden bound snatched a banana and retreated. Back on his branch he peeled it slowly. The tribe watched, inscrutable. Then sprang, simultaneously. Junior rammed the rest of the banana into his mouth, hurled the skin into the battle line, and retreated. A torrent of vervets leapt, somersaulting and gibbering, and the argument continued in the adjoining clump of trees. We finished our lunch.

The vervets visited us often, especially when we were not there. There were always traces of their visit: a glass upturned, a beer mat vanished, a towel discarded in the dust. Like naughty little boys, we missed them when they were not around.

One golden afternoon we drove the whole length of the Ilala Sala trail waist-high in jungle grass rippling for miles on either side. We saw not one ostrich but two, treading with their stately, heavy-footed gait and then suddenly breaking into a most un-birdlike gallop at our approach. Their comic departure convinced our younger son that the only place to travel for the rest of the journey was on the Land Rover roof, camera at the ready. A sudden urgent thumping of feet above would mean he had spotted something: an oryx, a lyre-horned deer, and once a family of wart hogs, tails suddenly alert in a warning signal as mother, father and three babies realised intruders were present. We dutifully slowed down and stopped.

We turned back towards camp as the sun set behind the twisted acacias. Our friendly dik-diks made for the water hole, and birds wheeled quietly back to their nests. There was a sudden hush before the small noises of evening. The first stars blinked.

At the camp the bonfire threw a flickering red glow. Sudden avalanches of brilliant sparks hissed from the great tree branches crackling in the flames. Nights by the river are full of sound. The barking of baboons on the other side of the river. The soft chorus of cicadas. Small ploppings in the water. If you looked carefully at the dark ripples, you could pick out the unmistakeable glint of crocodiles' eyes by the moonlight. The sky seemed very close. So did the crocodiles.

Outside the circle of firelight, the darkness waited. We kicked the last smouldering log, zipped the tent up snugly. And slept.

Bekeletch joined the family a little later, after a series of near disasters on my part with the Italian oven, which had a very limited temperature range ... either lukewarm or searing hot. Culinary efforts were further complicated by the altitude. Water had a different boiling point, sponge mixtures rose dramatically and then collapsed, and food would burn on the outside and then remain uncooked in the middle. Meal times tended to be a bit fraught, especially when visits of senior staff from New York Headquarters or Regional Office in Kampala involved home entertaining at short notice. So help was very welcome.

Bekeletch had two testimonials. One said she was lazy but

could manage washing and ironing. The second that she was honest and willing but spoke very limited English. My Amharic was even more limited than her English, so we agreed on a month's trial. The arrangement worked unbelievably well and her linguistic skills improved far more rapidly than mine. Bekeletch's shy smile and graceful young figure in immaculate white *shamma* brought a quiet feeling of harmony to the kitchen. She made Ababa Mingestu's mint tea for him every evening. She and Shumi got on splendidly, and even Simba treated her with guarded respect. She said she did not know any Western cooking, but managed to fix up a clay oven by the garden outhouse on which to bake her *injera* ... the Ethiopian bread which is used as an edible serving platter, all-purpose tablecloth, or just a snack. Spicy beef, chicken, or vegetables are laden on top as a communal dish, eaten by tearing off a piece of *injera* and wrapping it round a bite-sized morsel of the spicy filling, which is then conveyed neatly to one's mouth. This takes some practice. For guests it is usually served on top of an ingenious woven cane *injera* basket from which everyone helps themselves This also saves a lot of washing up. Wednesdays and Fridays are fasting days on which no chicken, meat, butter, eggs or milk are allowed; and so, of course, are the 60 days of Lent, and the 15-day period before the Feast of the Assumption. So one had to be aware of the date and appropriate food when entertaining Ethiopian guests. In this Bekeletch was a great help. And she watched carefully when I was cooking Western food and wrote down the ingredients and method of preparation very slowly in a treasured notebook. Once memorised, unlike me, she never seemed to forget anything.

Almost imperceptibly time went by. Bekeletch overcame her fear of the telephone and began to take messages if I was out. We fell into a routine where she would go back home every Saturday afternoon dressed in her best with her golden earrings enhancing her dark eyes, and return bright and early on Monday morning.

One Monday it was Shumi who brought the morning tea. He indicated that Bekeletch was unwell. 'You'd better talk to her,' said Alan helpfully as he set off for the office. So I did that. Bekeletch was in tears and unusually devious. Eventually I guessed the reason and wondered how to approach the subject tactfully. Finally I explained that if perhaps a baby was on the way it would help if she could tell us in good time for her to bring a friend to help her, show her how do to things in the house, and take over for a while until she was ready to come back. She hid her face and through the tears said she didn't know. Baby maybe three months, maybe six. Then the smile at last came back. And so it was that her pre-natal care, delivery and post-natal care were arranged with doctor friends at the Swedish hospital just down the road and cost us something like 500 Ethiopian dollars.

Johannes was a beautiful baby. When Bekeletch moved back in with him she brought a lad of about ten years with her to be his 'minder'. He cooked her *injera* and watched over the baby while she did the chores. Johannes grew chubby and even more handsome and Bekeletch had a new spring in her steps and light in her eyes. And when our two sons joined us for the eagerly awaited Christmas holidays – doubly popular because there were two Christmases to enjoy, the Ethiopian one coming some ten days after ours – they did not seem to need a language in common either. Those were especially happy days.

The foreign community in those days was richly varied. There were the Italians, who owned most of the garages and were skilled in all things mechanical. Italian food was widely available, and a stop for petrol would always include cooling, freshly made ice cream. On field trips, the remotest village would have tucked away some small bar supplying freshly baked rolls and delicious pasta and local beer to wash it down. On holiday weekends a favourite excursion was to the vineyards on the hill slopes where the grapes grew, for an Italian meal with locally produced wine. Not far down the same road an Austrian lady served Wiener-Schnitzel and Apfelstrudel in her little garden rampant with flowers and a collection of pet dogs. How she managed to combine the two was a mystery. But a meal on the shady lawn with the dogs playing puppy games was still relaxing.

The Armenian community were said to be descended from survivors of a Turkish massacre many years ago. They were skilled musicians, fashion designers, jewellers and hair stylists. We hired our piano from an Armenian who lived in the next compound to the most famous jeweller in town. And when we needed a replacement gas cylinder for our Italian oven (they always seemed to expire without warning at a time of maximum inconvenience), our Armenian friend who lived hard by the jeweller would deliver one at lightning speed on his (Italian) motorbike. So life as a *ferenji* did have some advantages.

Our dentist was Rumanian Jewish. He was not only highly skilled, he was gentle too, and an amazingly accomplished linguist. Listening to his telephone conversations in between drilling one's teeth was to experience a truly dramatic performance. He spoke fluent English, Amharic, German, French and Italian as well as his native tongue, and could switch from one to another whilst still concentrating on the dental problem in hand. For some reason I trusted him completely. For the first time in my life I actually looked forward to dental appointments. The surgery was in a tall grey stone house in a narrow street right at the top of the hill adjoining the vast Mercato area (said to be the largest market in the whole of Africa), where one could buy everything from local vegetables and raw meat or live chickens to hand-crafted silver crosses and leather goods, guns, ammunition, and air-force-style flying jackets for good measure. So there was always something new to discover.

Much, much later in our Ethiopian journey, at the beginning of the revolution, the schools and universities were closed. So the students took to the streets, some to throw stones, just at anything really. I had a dental appointment and set off in my little Fiat. Everything was very quiet. There was almost no traffic. I reached the tall house, to find an iron grille across the padlocked door to the surgery. Then Solomon appeared. He was the little street boy who always 'watched' my car for a small fee, thus preventing other street boys or the occasional petty thief from stealing windscreen wipers or hub caps. Solomon was very reliable. *'Tenastalign,'* he greeted me. 'Dentist?' I said yes, please. He took me by the hand up a side alley I had never noticed before, round another corner, and then pointed to a narrow iron outside staircase. 'Dentist,' he said confidently.

I thanked him, then said as an afterthought, 'Solomon ... have you been throwing stones?'

He grinned. 'Only *tinnish* ones.' *Tinnish* means 'little'.

Finally arriving at the door at the top of the steps, I was greeted by the great man himself. In the background his *mamita* was busy with a window cloth. I said, 'Cleaning windows? Today?'

He smiled. 'Of course. When my windows are about to be broken I like them to be clean. Will you lie back in the chair now please?'

When we finally and very reluctantly were posted away from Ethiopia, we managed to hand over the occupancy of the house, with Bekeletch, Shumi and Mingestu, to a newly arrived young English couple who liked dogs. So Simba stayed too. Apart from a few mild comments subsequently that Simba was protecting them from illegal intrusion, but sometimes seemed intent on discouraging their friends as well, we did not hear again for some years.

Then, quite by accident, Alan bumped into an Ethiopian office colleague a long way away from Addis – in Bangkok. They exchanged the usual lengthy formal greetings and courtesies. Then Ato Abate gave one of his huge grins. 'Your dog Simba,' he said. 'He is fine. He survived the revolution. Only last week I visited my friend who is a doctor in Addis. He had just been treating a patient Simba had bitten.'

The Ethiopians themselves are unique. A warrior race, proud, with a natural dignity, their rulers believed to be descended from King Solomon and the Queen of Sheba, they do not consider themselves 'Africans'. They are indeed many races. Their country lies in the Horn of Africa, bordered by the Sudan, Somalia and Kenya, harbouring the source of the Blue Nile, and bisected by the Great Rift Valley. Their womenfolk are uniquely beautiful, with the huge dark eyes of the traditional religious paintings, graceful in their hand-woven Muslim *shammas*, a white garment with full skirt, and a long shawl draped round the shoulders and head, rather like a shorter sari, with delicate hand-embroidered border. The men are tall and handsome. The more Westernised, in the towns, wear European dress except for festivals and holy days, when they too, like the countrymen, wear white muslin – loose shirts and tight gaiters wound round the legs, and long white shawls to wrap around the head when the sun gives way to night's chill – looking always ready to leap on horseback in the style of their forefathers in the days when the capital city was a moving camp. During our stay you could still buy a horse more cheaply than the saddle. Small boys seemed to ride bareback as early as they learned to walk.

The Shoans in the highlands around Addis Ababa were landowners and farmers of the rich volcanic soil. The Guraghes, sturdy and darker-hued, skilled in felling eucalyptus trees in the groves so plentiful around the city, were familiar neighbours. They would shin barefoot up the trunk to lop away the top leaves, then, gripping with their toes, sever the top of the tree, then progressively a second and third cut would leave a clean stump. Each length of wood had its purpose, from telephone poles and supports for roofs of the thatched *tukuls* to humble tools and walking sticks.

The Arussi lived in the lower climes of the Rift Valley lakes, and were distinguishable by their intricately plaited hair greased with butter. Different again were the Afar nomadic tribes of the Danakil desert, who moved with their tents, and the camels whose milk and blood were their staple food. The young men were tall and fine-featured, dressed in loin cloths slung with their curved daggers, the women barebreasted and strikingly beautiful. One encountered them at the weekly market at Awash Station on the way to the

National Wildlife Park, but it was wiser not to take photographs of the womenfolk.

Then there were the Eritreans, who were handsome and skilled at everything and now have their own country.

The Rift Valley lakes each had their own special beauty: the glory of pink flamingoes on lakes Shalla and Abiata, the wildness of lake Awassa with its fishing eagles swooping over the dark waves at sunrise, and Langano, which was free of the snails that carried bilharzia and therefore safe for swimming. There was a small hotel run by an Italian of indeterminate age. He looked as though he had been there forever. Accommodation consisted of small bedrooms with attached mini-bathrooms on a ridge overlooking the lake where hippos lived, but one seldom met them. A tribe of baboons was sometimes encountered on a stroll round the lakeshore after an early morning swim, and I would beat a hasty retreat. Otherwise they kept themselves very much to themselves.

Flanking the black sand beach was the 'dining room', which supplied breakfast and light meals. I remember most vividly the 'spaghetti with three sauces' (red, green and yellow) and the giant plastic bottles of tomato ketchup for use with everything. This was very popular with the younger generation who came down from Addis for Ethiopian Christmas in January. There were Italians, Greeks, British, Ethiopians and Armenians, and the UN families, who were even more diverse. Our sons' particular cronies at that time were from Norway, New Zealand and Korea. At meal times ketchup battles were regular and usually friendly.

As darkness fell, they all gathered on the beach with their tents and sleeping bags. There was a shack by the water's edge supplying snacks, soft drinks and cans of Ethiopian beer. One little Arussi boy had appointed himself bringer of kindling for the bonfire and would run errands to the shack. It was all very spontaneous and comradely as only teenagers can be when their world is young and the moon is bright. The soft strumming of guitars blended with the tiny waves lapping and the sweet wafting smell of acacia wood. And the night wind was always warm.

The end of the school holidays came all too quickly, with last-minute packing and the hurtling journey to the airport, then the last frantic waving as the sturdy Ethiopian Airlines plane nosed into a clear blue sky and disappeared slowly from sight, and suddenly life felt very empty.

That was the downside of being a 'UN wife'.

The after-Christmas gloom seemed to weigh more heavily, that last year. There were fears of crop failure where the little rains had failed, rumours of cattle dying in the Lower Valley, and a restlessness about in town. Alan disappeared to attend board meetings in Kampala, and I invited all the office local staff females for lunch as usual when he was away. They enjoyed it, and so did Bekeletch, because it gave her a chance to display her now very expert cooking, I got to know about their lives and their problems, and they seemed to trust me. Besides, it made a welcome break for us all. Those were anxious times.

That was when the serval cat startled me. A sound from the sliding doors in the lounge at nightfall revealed a startlingly close pair of eyes in a whiskered face pressed against the glass. A silent shape finally disappeared into the shadows. I tried to concentrate on reading. Before bed I opened the kitchen door to make an Ovaltine nightcap, only to be confronted by a large rat, who stood his ground, unblinking. I retreated without my Ovaltine. I think I slept fairly well after securing the bedroom door extra carefully, but woke early to unusually loud noises from the kitchen. Bekeletch had climbed on to the little kitchen table clutching her skirt round her ankles, and was screaming, while Shumi was engaged in furious combat with a horribly mobile and very angry rat, which he was belaying with our plastic fly swot. I retreated hastily. Shumi killed the rat, then opened the oven door to show me the chewed remnants of the electrical wiring behind the rotisserie section. Suddenly I didn't feel like breakfast.

Salvation came with a totally unexpected phone call. It was from a friend at the Embassy. She said a firm of British consultants, engaged on a feasibility study for construction of a dam in the Awash River, were having problems with typing and assembling the team's reports for mailing to their head office in the UK. Did I want to help? She gave me the telephone number of the project manager, who asked when I could get down to their office to see the paperwork involved. There seemed no time like the present.

The Awash Valley Authority compound was on the far side of town. Beyond the compound walls was a view of Addis Ababa with its winding, hilly streets rivalling the more famous viewpoint from Entoto. The office consisted of three small rooms with adjoining bathroom. When I arrived, the project manager occupied a desk overflowing with paper. Most of it seemed to be hand-written weekly reports from the team, comprising geologists, soil surveyors, an agronomist and a seismologist, who were engaged in the groundwork of a feasibility study for a dam construction at Tendaho, where the Awash River winds its way towards its disappearance in the Danakil desert. They were housed in caravans in the Lower Valley adjoining Afar country.

Eyes met across a pile of assorted documents and the project manager said, 'Can you type?', then asked when I could start. There seemed only one answer. He showed me the ancient typewriter, sharing a small desk in the adjoining room with yet more paper. Foot room was limited by plastic containers filled with water samples, large and small sacks of soil samples, and odd but precious boxes and packing materials and hessian, all sure to be useful one day. The typewriter rattled away splendidly, but it was comforting to have my little portable for back-up.

Australian colleagues of the United Nations Development Program worked in offices just across the courtyard and possessed a teleprinter, which was handy in emergencies. Cars and Land Rovers rushed precipitously round the narrow bend to screech to a halt a few yards from the window. Dusty vehicles would disgorge equally dusty young field team members.

One Scottish geologist had earned local fame by always working dressed in the kilt, on the verge of the hottest place on earth. I marvelled at their dedication.

There was never a dull or idle moment, but small cups of thick black coffee would appear on a rusty tray at regular intervals. The office messenger was more than generous with sugar. Or for the same ten Ethiopian cents one could have a murky glass of tea flavoured with cloves. I found the main problem was locating anyone anywhere else at any given time. With transport problems, frequently defunct generators (at their end) and disappearing radio operators (at our end), communication with the survey team was at best problematical. But the sun always shone and the progress reports began to meet mail deadlines. I still wonder whether the dam ever became a reality...

As the survey drew to a close, I helped inventory the caravans in the Lower Valley. We left early morning for Dubti in a little Piper Cub which had to report back to the control tower at Bole airport by sunset. There were no night landing facilities. So it was a busy day. But time to see my first fumarole, and the *teff* – the Ethiopian equivalent of wheat, used also as animal fodder – still struggling to survive under a blazing sun. But there was an all-pervading smell of dead cattle on the drive back to the tiny airstrip.

Very slowly the clouds of the revolution closed in. There were road blocks of sandbags manned by army and police checking ID cards on all the intersections leading to the centre of town. Where we lived in the Old Airport area there were rumours of mounting unrest and confusion among sections of the armed services. When the rains failed again, there were more beggars by the roadside. Most rural families in Ethiopia relied on their cow or goat to provide milk and meat. There was no need to kill the animal, one just carved off pieces of living warm flesh, laced the wound with dung, and usually the animal lived to feed another day, when the grass and scrub were green and lush. Without rain the vegetation died, the water holes dried up and so did the animals' milk. When famine crept in, the animals like their owners grew weaker, and no longer lived to feed another day.

But the country folk still believed the good Lord would send rain when the time was ripe. They were patient in their waiting, and the churches were always full. Many of the Coptic priests were among the first to join with the 'barefoot doctors' (young medical students who were trained under a joint government/UNICEF-funded programme to perform simple eye operations and vaccinations, and diagnose and treat minor health problems) and the relief agencies, to minister to the growing numbers of refugees.

Civil war was simmering too. Ever since the annexation of Eritrea after the Italian invasion of 1935 there had been disputes over sovereignty and border skirmishes. The Eritreans fiercely defended their right to the Red Sea port of Massawa. Apart from the formerly French port of Djibouti, now independent, the only access to the sea was the small port of Assab, approached by a desert road. Conscription left the land untended as the men were sent away to fight. Without rain the seeds that were sown died. Moving in search of food, the women grubbed for roots as the famine spread.

A child died at the end of our lane when cholera struck. The family and friends gathered, the men to drink and talk, the women to sit in silence and mourn. Inside the little house with its roof of straw, a dim light licked at the shadows and outlined the figures wrapped in white shawls, flickered in watchful dark eyes. We left our gate light on for them that night.

Our four-year assignment came to an end. The familiar routine of packing and disposing ensued, but this time it was different. I was in the quiet study trying to concentrate on packing lists with my little portable, when Bekeletch asked nervously if I was busy. They wanted to talk with me in the kitchen. She was in tears, and Shumi blowing his nose furiously on what must have been a borrowed handkerchief. Why were we going? I tried to explain. Both the Embassy housing officer and the landlord had agreed to the new family moving in, and they wanted them both, and of course Mingestu, to stay on and help look after the house. All would be well. But none of us knew ... how could we?

We flew out to Nairobi on Saturday, November 23, 1974. It was a glorious sunny day. Addis Ababa, literally 'New Flower' shrank far below into a delicate miniature in pearl grey, looked so beautiful and somehow fragile that it hurt. We were not to know that before darkness fell that night the Prime Minister, the Emperor's favourite grandson and most of the cabinet ministers – some 60 persons in all – were to be 'executed by orders of the Military Government for crimes committed against the Ethiopian people and for attempts to disrupt the country's popular movement. The persons had been buried and relatives were not allowed to ask for their remains'. The press statement when we saw it later was brief and to the point. All we knew then was the deep sadness of parting. We remembered Bekeletch and her quiet farewell, her dark eyes clouded. 'Your family is as my family. Governments do not care about little people. But you love as we love you. Why do you go?' Her hands were folded, young brown hands, over her new white *shamma*. Johannes crawled round her shapely bare feet. '*Tenastalign*, God be with you.' 'And with you.' We hoped He was.

Now there was another famine, described as 'of biblical proportions'. Newspapers and newsreels in England featured the same quiet desolation and suffering as the weakest died first. Again the relief agencies did all they could to help, and people were generous in their response to appeals for funds. One poster appeared everywhere. It was a black and white portrayal of two hands, folded over a piece of cloth. The hands were wrinkled, had known youth in passing, and a lifetime of toil. Now they were passive, not without beauty and dignity. The cloth was rough and the colour of cotton spun from the flax in the fields, or wool from the household sheep or goat. It brought memories flooding back...

The road to Debre Lebanos was always lined with beggars. The grey stone monastery was a place of pilgrimage. The rich came in their cars or on horseback and gave alms generously, so it was a gathering place for the lame and the blind and the very poor. The blind stared through eyes crusted with flies, each guided by a young boy on whose shoulder one ageing hand would rest lightly, trustingly. The lame and the crippled and the lepers squatted in the dust, hands folded round their begging bowls. Mothers suckled strangely listless babies, oblivious to the busy clustered flies. Their hands cradled the fragile burdens, tender and passive.

Ten years had passed. From our cosy side of the world we had thought of them, worried, tried to send word. But no answer. Only the bleak snatches of newsreel and now another, worse famine. Little Johannes, God willing, would be 11 years old.

How could we still feel stricken ... over a poster?

17

Farewell to Chosun

Alan's last posting before retirement was back to Korea, where we rented a tiny house in the former Scandinavian Medical Centre in downtown Seoul with a wee garden gate opening on to the compound lawns and flowering trees. The adjoining twin house was occupied by Swedish Army officers when they arrived for weekends from the DMZ (demilitarised zone) on the 39th Parallel on rest and recreation leave, so life was never dull.

In May 1981, Alan was awarded a medal and citation of the Order of Civil Merit for 'his valuable dedication and service which has gained for him the appreciation and admiration of the Korean people', presented by President Chun Doo Hwan at a ceremony in the Blue House. This was a great honour for him, and very lucky for me, because I happened to attend the Medical Centre hospital on the same day for acupuncture treatment on a painfully swollen hand. Expecting a long wait (it was a very busy hospital), I was suddenly greeted by the senior doctor asking if I were related to the Alan McBain who had just been honoured by the President? On my assent a cubicle was found immediately, and the treatment was painless and instantly effective. I promised not to do any more single-handed house- clearing operations.

Life in between packing became a heartwarming series of farewell receptions and dinners given by Ministers and other Korean friends, who took enormous trouble to show their genuine affection for someone who loved their country too. The evening I remember most clearly was given by our old friend Mr Kang, formerly housing manager of the Itaewon complex and now manager of the prestigious new Shilla Hotel. There were flowers by every plate, the food was absolutely delicious and even the matchboxes were printed with our names. It was a memory to treasure when his Christmas card arrived unfailingly every year in faraway Kent.

The entire office staff came to see us off at the airport and I think we were all in tears. We went home the long way, first to Tokyo, where we breakfasted with Alan's old friend Mr Masanari, who sold him a new camera. I ordered some varifocal glasses at an optician he recommended – much cheaper in those days than the UK price – which they promised to deliver to us in Geneva, and to my surprise they were waiting for us when we arrived. Nick had just finished a year after sixth form as an exchange student through the English Speaking Union with a reciprocal college in Connecticut, which to his delight had actually adjoined the Appalachian trail, kindling what remains a lifelong interest in orienteering and camping. We arranged to meet him at Miami airport en route to Hawaii, and by some miracle as we negotiated the myriad twists and turns of walkways and scurrying passengers, a familiar figure emerged unhurried from yet another tunnel with a casual 'Hi'. With his haversack slung over his shoulders, he seemed to have grown taller. It was so good to see him again.

We had happy memories of our earlier short holiday in Honolulu with both the boys, before Hawaii became the newest State of America. Skyscrapers were few and far between, the beaches golden and uncrowded, and the sea was turquoise flecked with green where the breakers curled.

This time around, we found the Halekulani Hotel unchanged. And our friend the lifeguard. He and Nicky were soon back in the water with surfboards, Alan relaxed in the cool of our rondavel and I stretched out in the shade of a palm tree on the beach and went to sleep. I woke to find the sun had moved, I had a very sore back and legs, and a voice said 'Lady, you sure have scorched your arse.' It was none other than our lifeguard friend, who produced some healing Hawaiian coconut oil and smoothed it in gently. So all was well. Time as always went far too quickly, and the leis we were given at the airport were still fresh as we left on the now familiar road to catch our plane.

The Hawaiians are an incredibly handsome race, the women folk beautiful with their dark eyes and long black hair always bedecked with lotus flowers, and the mixed population in Honolulu of Chinese, Polynesian, Korean and Westerners all seemed to get along so well. Perhaps it was something to do with the beauty of the islands and the serenity of the soft guitar melodies and traditional dancing, all linked to the richness of nature surrounding them. Either way, to us it was heaven.

To home and Thanet in September again.

EPILOGUE

I suppose everyone has their own Thanet. Mine was always the island on the other side of the water, and the voyage of discovery spanned a lifetime of changing times, changing moods. Unpredictable, like the sea.

The enchantment began early on, as a child, at Thorpe Bay on the Essex coast. It seemed a long walk from our home in Prittlewell, but my father thought the water was cleaner. The waves lapped icy fingers round my legs as I trod the cold sharp pebbles underfoot and he said, 'Get your shoulders underneath. Then it won't feel so cold.' Of course he was right. When I emerged spluttering and feeling very brave after the early morning swimming lesson, father would buy me a mug of hot chocolate from the beach stall. Wrapped in a large towel, I would watch for the first smudge of sunlight, and catch a glimpse of shining white on the other side, across the mud flats of the Thames estuary. That was where the cliffs of Kent began.

My first trip by paddle steamer was both fearful and exciting, with the dark water splashing through the slatted boards of Southend pier, and then the inching down the gangplank to the heaving deck of the *Crested Eagle*. After a shrill blast of the funnel, the pier moved backwards, seagulls wheeled overhead, and we bobbed gently to the throb of engines towards the miracle of white cliffs crowned with downland grass and rooted in smooth pale yellow sand. And Margate pier.

When I returned it was to a Thanet in wartime. The

beaches were empty of people, but starfish and tiny shrimps still swam in the rock pools and the cliffs were still gleaming white. We Wrens had moved from Dover with our MTB flotilla after D Day. The little boats slid out of harbour under cover of darkness, the crew at attention in their seagoing white jerseys.

Moonlight was bad luck. Our thoughts went with them, fingers crossed for their safe return. The skies were alive with the beauty and horror of bursting shells, and bright orange balls of fire where the pompoms traced zigzag patterns across the inky blackness.

Mornings were always sunlit, with the sky chasing puffs of cloud as we walked along Royal Terrace to the base. Meals were mostly stew and chocolate pudding or plum duff and pale watery custard, but we still always seemed to be hungry. A little café we passed down the zigzag steps could always be relied upon to supply eggs and chips. It is still there, but the menu is different. Then they were seagulls' eggs, fresh and golden-yolked, and tasting ever so slightly of fish. Now when the descendants of that colony clomp over our roof in hobnail boots on bright mornings I hope they bear no grudge.

Coming back for the third time with two small sons on home leaves, we discovered the seaweed-slippery slopes of Colmans stairs, and the peacetime delights of dodgem cars speeding round their tracks in my old naval base turned into an amusement arcade, The miniature railway on Margate pier was working once more, piloted by the old one-armed driver. Nicholas was as fascinated by the one empty sleeve as he was by the turning wheels and cogs, and I was always afraid he was going to ask about it in his piercing voice. But he never did. He just watched it carefully.

Birchington in the late fifties was still a village edging into the fields towards Minnis Bay. There were blackberries in the hedgerows and mushrooms in the autumn fields. Returning from a day away, the Thanet Way felt like coming home.

Retirement was not Alan's favourite option. I don't think it was with any of the 'old guard' who remained friends over the years. But he kept busy, helping to start the East Kent

UNICEF Support Group, which grows in strength and dedicated membership, and had time for the music he loved, at last with his own piano. We were both lucky to have a home to 'settle' in and entertain old colleagues passing through, and I revelled in my own garden to dig. The years slipped past at an alarming speed but the world seems to have changed very little. The spotlight of the media occasionally notices the continued plight of the Karen peoples of Burma and the inhuman treatment of Nobel Prize winner Aung San Suu Kyi, their elected president. Civil war and famine never seem very far from Ethiopia and Eritrea, now separate but still of the same kingdom. The two Koreas are happily now working towards a peace treaty but it will take time – perhaps too much for one lifetime – for divided families to be united. But looking back from the Millennium, life has been special and we have been so very lucky to be part of it all.

When it comes to settling, there is a lot to be said for familiar gulls hovering round the chimney, sand in your shoes, and sunsets over the Goodwins. And the winter hush round Dumpton Gap.